Scapegoat General

SCAPEGOAT GENERAL

*The Story of Major General
Benjamin Huger, C.S.A.*

Jeffrey L. Rhoades

ARCHON BOOKS 1985

*The paper in this book meets the guidelines for performance and
durability of the Committee on Production Guidelines for Book
Longevity of the Council on Library Resources.*

Library of Congress Cataloging-in-Publication Data

Rhoades, Jeffrey L., 1945–
  Scapegoat general.

Bibliography: p.
Includes index.
  1. Huger, Benjamin, 1805–1877.   2. Generals—United States—Biography.
3. United States. Army— Biography.   4. Confederate States of America.
Army—Biography.   5. Malvern Hill, Battle of, 1862.
6. Peninsular Campaign, 1862.   I. Title.
E467.1.H883R48 1985   973.7'3'0924 [B]   85-18530
ISBN 0-208-02069-1 (alk. paper)

Printed in the United States of America

Designed by Marie-Louise Scull

To My Mother

Contents

Illustrations

1. *Introduction*

Born in Charleston, South Carolina, on 22 November 1805, Benjamin Huger (ū-jē) belonged to an old French Huguenot family. His paternal great-great-grandfather, Daniel Huger, had left London, France, and settled in South Carolina in 1696. In the early years of American history, Daniel's descendants served with distinction in civil and military employment in the state and Federal governments.

Ben's father, Francis Kinloch (kin-lăw) Huger, received an M.D. degree from the University of Pennsylvania, although he did not practice medicine. He served two terms in the state legislature and was an artillery officer in the War of 1812. His father, Major Benjamin Huger, at his summer home on North Island, near Georgetown, South Carolina, entertained the Marquis de Lafayette and his party when they landed in America to offer assistance to the revolutionary cause. While a young man, Francis was engaged in the chivalrous enterprise of attempting to rescue Lafayette from confinement in the Austrian prison of Olmutz. The fame of the courageous youth, hailed by Lafayette as his "heroic deliverer," spread throughout Europe and America.

Ben's mother, Harriott Lucas Huger, was the second daughter of Thomas Pinckney. The Pinckneys, like the Hugers, were among the cream of southern aristocracy. Among the many highlights of his life, Thomas Pinckney

1

created the historic treaty between the United States and Spain known as the Pinckney Treaty, served two terms as governor of South Carolina, and was a major general in the War of 1812. His brother, Major General Charles Cotesworth Pinckney, was the United States minister to France who became world-famous in the XYZ Affair and was a framer and signer of the Constitution of the United States. Their mother, Eliza Lucas Pinckney, was put in charge of her father's three South Carolina plantations at the age of sixteen; and from her knowledge of the indigo plant and her experiments with flax, hemp, and silk culture, she aided materially in promoting economic independence for her state. She had done so much to promote economic independence in the colonies that when she died, President George Washington, at his own request, served as a pallbearer at her funeral.

No doubt greatly influenced by his military ancestry, young Huger dreamed of the day when he too would don a proud uniform. That day came surprisingly soon. In 1821, at the age of only fifteen, he was appointed to the United States Military Academy at West Point, New York. As a cadet, he was a gentle looking, handsome boy with bright blue eyes and dark brown hair. Among his classmates of future fame were Jefferson Davis and Robert Anderson.

While at the academy, Ben met Lafayette for the first time. The honored guest of the nation, accompanied by a son and Huger's father in his entourage, was on a four-month tour of the United States and made a planned stop at West Point in 1824. All academic exercises were suspended for the day. When the general arrived, a battery of artillery fired a national salute; and the corps of cadets paraded in review in front of the quarters of the superintendent, Brevet Lieutenant Colonel Sylvanus Thayer, who would become known to history as the "Father of the Military Academy."

Huger's record as a cadet was most outstanding. A gifted student, he was on the honor roll in every course of study. He received instruction in artillery and fencing; and his academic courses included mathematics, French, philosophy, engineering, tactics, chemistry and minerology, geography, history, and natural law. He especially excelled in tactics. He received surprisingly few demerits. Of these, one offense was repeated at least four times during his cadetship—visiting during study hours. His high class standing entitled him to his choice of corps. Following in the footsteps of his father, he chose artillery. He graduated while still a teenager in 1825 eighth in a class of thirty-seven members as a second lieutenant in the Third Artillery.

For the next three years, Huger was detailed on topographical duty. In 1828 he was permitted to go to Europe on leave of absence for improvement in professional and general knowledge. He went first to Paris, where he visited Lafayette frequently and conversed at length with the elderly general. While in London, he met the Duke of Wellington, the English general who had defeated Napoleon at Waterloo. There also he saw Sir Walter Scott, world-renowned Scottish novelist and poet, of whom he wrote:

> I met him standing in the lobby [of Parliament] talking to a gentleman[;] and you may depend I took a good look at him, tho' in his countenance I could perceive nothing remarkable. He is a good[-]sized man, apparently about 50[,] with a round snub of a nose in his face and very lame in the right leg. The court room [where Scott was a clerk] is always filled with persons who come to look at him. The ladies have a very great curiosity this way and will do any thing to get possession of the pen with which he has been writing. He is much more sought after than any [other] great man I have ever seen.[1]

Returning to Paris, Huger's first care was to call on Lafayette, who had been ill when he had left France for England. He was pleased to find the general in excellent health and spirits. Through the general's influence, he was able to attend a session of the Chamber of Deputies, the governing body of France. As it was Huger's intenion to tour the country, Lafayette wrote numerous letters of introduction to high officials at places the lieutenant expressed the desire to visit, making the latter's travels much easier. After his tour of France, Huger visited parts of Ireland, Germany, and Italy. He returned to the United States in 1830 as a perfectionist in horsemanship and fencing, with an increased knowledge in artillery, engineering, chemistry, and mathematics.

On his return home, Huger was placed on recruiting service and then in the garrison of Fort Trumbull, Connecticut. He now felt prepared to crown an unusual courtship with marriage. His courtship was indeed unusual; the bride-to-be was Elizabeth Celestine (sĕl-ĕ-stēn') Pinckney—his first cousin. Celly, as she was called, was the elder of two children (both daughters) of Colonel Thomas Pinckney, Jr., Ben's uncle. She had light brown hair; and her sparkling, deep blue eyes were of such a hue that her middle name had been derived from "celestial."

Colonel Pinckney opposed the consanguineous marriage from the start. When it became evident that dissuasive arguments had no favorable effect, threats were made. If the couple were wed, he warned at length, he would write a new will and leave them both completely disinherited. But in spite of threats and ill feelings, Huger married his cousin on 17 February 1831. As promised, the wealthy patriarch cut them out of his will.

The colonel was not only disturbed by the marriage, which he probably considered incestuous, but also by the possibility that his daughter could suddenly become an unhappy widow. For this reason, he offered his son-in-law nephew a cotton plantation if he would resign from the army. Huger sternly refused the offer and later declared that he would never receive or accept one dollar of his father-in-law's property in any shape. Actually Colonel Pinckney, in his own way, had Celly's best interest at heart.

When the ordnance department was reorganized as a separate branch of the army in 1832, Huger, still a second lieutenant, was selected by a board of officers for special appointment to the rank of captain in the new corps. Before this time, the ordnance department had been staffed by artillery officers. The department was charged with the design, manufacture, storage, distribution, and repair of weapons of all kinds, their equipment, and ammunition.

In his new capacity, Huger was placed in command of the arsenal under construction at star-shaped Fort Monroe, Virginia. During his service there, five children were born to the family. In 1839 the arsenal commander became a member of the ordnance board of the War Department, no doubt a result of the knowledge he had gained in Europe, as the board had charge of considering and recommending all new inventions and improvements in every matter concerning ordnance. In 1840 Huger was selected by Secretary of War Joel R. Poinsett as a member of a commission to be sent abroad to study European methods of warfare and to visit the foundries and military establishments throughout Europe. He returned to the United States in 1841 as an expert in the field of ordnance and bore an important part in the reorganization and improvement of the system of artillery, which became known as the Model 1840 family of weapons, and of the general armament and equipment of the army.

During the Mexican War, Huger served as the chief of both ordnance and artillery to Winfield Scott, the general-in-chief of the United States armies, and commanded a siege train, which consisted of batteries of heavy artillery and mortars and wagons of ordnance supplies. The object of Major General Scott's expedition was to end the war by capturing the enemy's capital, Mexico City. To accomplish this, the army was to strike a decisive blow at the key seaport of Vera Cruz and march inland some 270 miles.

In the first major amphibious landing in the history of the United States Army, Scott's troops landed near Vera Cruz with little opposition on 9 March 1847. After the city was invested, Huger planted mortar batteries from his siege train and opened fire on the twenty-second. Vera Cruz, the most heavily armed city in the Western Hemisphere, surrendered after three weeks of siege, the result of the moral effect of Huger's fire on the civilian population. The mortars hurled more than three thousand shells, over a quarter of a million pounds of exploding metal. In many instances, whole streets laid in rubble with deep ridges ploughed into them and their pavements thrown up in crumbled heaps. Domes and steeples tumbled into the streets below. Buildings fell in ruins. The southwest quarter of the city, subjected to Huger's heaviest fire, was completely destroyed. Probably most extraordinary was that Huger was working with what was considered a totally inadequate siege train. Only two of his seven ordnance ships had arrived by the time the siege ended.

After the American victories at Cerro Gordo and Contreras

and Churubusco, Scott's army prepared to attack the fortifications of Molino del Rey and Chapultepec, which barred the way to the capital. When the Americans overran the Mexican battery at Molino del Rey, Huger took over the guns, reversed their direction of fire, and blasted the retreating Mexicans until they were out of range. Scott's troops then took position against Chapultepec, a rocky hill on the edge of Mexico City. During a fourteen-hour cannonade by his heavy artillery on 12 September, Huger attempted to force the Mexican garrison to retire. When this could not be realized, an assault on the fortification was ordered for the following day.

Huger's cannonade resumed on 13 September to prepare the way for infantry forces to storm the hill. Huger received orders from Scott to cease fire, and the stormers advanced to the attack. When they began to ascend the hill, a devastating infantry and artillery fire suddenly opened at them. The frantic ranks, unable to continue forward and unwilling to retreat, huddled among brush and boulders and fired almost vertically at the parapets far above. The vanguard, being not more than fifty yards from the Mexican works on the hillside, was in a state of panic. Some of the men were too scared to fire their muskets. Officers and men fell in dreadful slaughter. The attack had failed.

Against previous orders, Huger reopened his fire just over the heads of the stormers. He was painfully aware that a misdirected round that hit one of them would ruin him, but he accepted the risk. Within a matter of minutes, his batteries silenced the enemy's fire to the extent that the order to charge was given to the storming columns. With renewed spirit and vigor, the stormers continued their advance, firing their small arms and throwing hand grenades. Some of them told Huger after the battle that his whizzing shot and shells sounded as if they nearly touched their service caps. Columns of Mexican infantry made several desperate attempts to reinforce their comrades in the works, but each time they were hurled back by Huger's fire. The closer the attackers came to the Mexican works, however, the more increased were Huger's chances of a court-martial and the loss of his career. Yet he continued firing until the Americans became mingled with the Mexicans.

The stormers soon reached the western walls of

Chapultepec, mounted scaling ladders, and engaged in desperate hand-to-hand fighting. Overpowered by the unexpected cannonade and the audacity of the attackers, the Mexicans gave way or fled and surrendered by the hundreds. The triumphant American army entered the capital on 14 September; Huger celebrated with Scott and staff in the National Palace, also known as the Halls of Montezuma.

Scott, in his official report, referred to Huger as "an officer distinguished by every kind of merit."[2] Before the Mexican commander in chief, Antonio Lopez de Santa Anna, departed his country in exile, he surrendered his sword to Scott, who returned it with equal military courtesy. Santa Anna was so touched by the extraordinary favor that he removed a pair of gold-inlaid spurs from his boots and handed them to his conqueror. Scott in turn gave them to Huger as a symbol of his admiration and personal affection.

Huger was honored by both the army and his native state. He received the successive brevets[3] of major, lieutenant colonel, and colonel for "gallant and meritorious conduct" at Vera Cruz, Molino del Rey, and Chapultepec.[4] Of the many hundreds of officers who had participated in Scott's campaign, only four were awarded as many as three brevets; and of the four, Huger was the only one to be brevetted for every battle in which he fought. He was also awarded a Sword of Honor by South Carolina for his skill and valor in battle and in recognition of the honor which his career cast on his state.

On his return from Mexico, Huger resumed command of the Fort Monroe Arsenal, and from 1849 to 1851, again served on the ordnance board. As a member of the board, he was instrumental in devising a complete system of instructions for siege, garrison, seacoast, and mountain artillery. In 1851 he was selected to serve as superintendent of the Harpers Ferry Armory in Virginia (later West Virginia). His next post, in 1854, was the Pikesville Arsenal, near Baltimore, where he assumed the dual role of arsenal commander and inspector of United States foundries. When he was promoted to major of ordnance in 1855, he never dreamed that, in a relatively short time, a new republic would be begging him to accept a generalship, along with supreme command of its army.

2. *"God Help Us"*

In the South, where Federal power had long been viewed with
suspicion, the majority stood loyally by their states rather
than by the government of the Union. Always leading the
other southern states in secessionist sentiment was South
Carolina. Huger could have vividly recalled his earliest
recognition of sectional discord. The year was 1828, and the in-
dustrialized North was imposing on its agricultural neighbors
of the South a tariff so harsh that it became known as the
"Tariff of Abominations." Huger, then on his first European
tour, read in a Paris newspaper that South Carolina was in
uproarious opposition to the tariff, that the southern states
would secede from the Union, and that a civil war would result.
"I suppose the opposition to it [the tariff] among you must be
very strong," he wrote to his father, "but a good deal must be
allowed for their European imaginations." He asked Lafayette
in conversation if the general had heard that the states were
going to separate. The elderly man who had done so much for
the cause of American independence replied that he had heard
during the past fifty years that the states would secede but
was himself beginning to be rather incredulous on the subject
as it had become an old story.[1] In a letter written to Huger a
short time later, Lafayette took a more sober view:

I have in time received your kind answer inclosing the extract of a letter from your father[,] whose expressed sentiments are truly worthy of him, and I wish they were adopted by some of my friends in your part of the Union.[2] Not that I blame their opposition, however warm it may be, to any measure they think injurious to the country in general and to their own state, but the principle of the Confederacy [of the Union] is so sacred, so vital to all, so important to each & every one of the states and to the cause of [humanity], that a threat of dissolution is not an argument to be employed in discussion, the less so as I hope that those who make use of it would be among the first to deprecate the execution if matters were to come [to] . . . that deplorable & ruinous crisis.[3]

By 1860 the situation was critical. Late in October, Brevet Lieutenant General Scott anticipated that there would be a secession of one or more of the Democratic southern states in the event of the election of Republican presidential candidate Abraham Lincoln. He believed that the nine vacant or weakly garrisoned Federal forts in the South, those in Charleston harbor among them, were in danger of seizure by secessionists and urged President James Buchanan to garrison them strongly at once.

Buchanan was opposed. The United States Army, a scant force of slightly more than sixteen thousand soldiers, was spread thin, protecting a vast territory. Besides, reinforcing the forts would inflame the southern excitement which he was trying to pacify. The president, like most northerners, underestimated the growing crisis and would continue to try to maintain the balance of peace between the North and the South.

As Scott had anticipated, the election of Lincoln incited South Carolina to seek separation from the Union and become an independent republic. The four forts in Charleston harbor— Johnson, Moultrie, Sumter, and Castle Pinckney—were Federal property. The Charlestonians believed, however, that the defenses in their harbor belonged to their state. After secession, the new republic would send commissioners to Washington to negotiate for them. In the meantime, the state threatened that any strengthening of them by the national government would be met with unrestrained violence. Thus the forts became a symbol. To the North, they represented the preservation of the Union, to the South, a threat to peaceable secession.

The situation in Charleston harbor was precarious. The garrison at Moultrie was insufficient, the fort itself indefensible. Fort Johnson on James Island had since been abandoned, Fort Sumter was vacant, and Castle Pinckney was occupied by only an ordnance sergeant and his family. A congressional appropriation had been previously made for the repair of Moultrie and the completion of Sumter. Shortly after Captain John G. Foster of the engineers hired a corps of stonemasons and mechanics from Charleston and Baltimore and began work, the Carolinians voiced opposition to the engineering work being done on "their" property, some even regarding the work as aggression.

Not unexpectedly, a sensitive spot in the city was the United States arsenal, commanded by Captain Francis C. Humphreys, a military storekeeper, with fourteen men. After dark on 8 November, the commandant of Fort Moultrie attempted without success to obtain needed ammunition and supplies from the arsenal. Four days later twenty South Carolina militiamen were posted at the arsenal, and Captain Humphreys was told by the lieutenant in charge that the state was tendering the detachment as a guard in case of an insurrection among the slaves. But while the guard would prevent slaves from stealing any of the twenty-two thousand muskets stored in the arsenal, the act could be interpreted as a suggestion on the part of the state that Federal soldiers as well as slaves would have difficulty in removing arms or supplies from the depot, thus crippling the small garrison at Moultrie.

In order to safeguard the United States property against the angry citizens without increasing their wrath, Secretary of War John B. Floyd viewed the problem as a diplomatic rather than a military one. He determined to send two goodwill ambassadors, instead of reinforcements, to serve as a gesture to show the state the amicable intentions of the government. Floyd sent Major Robert Anderson of the First Artillery to Moultrie to take charge of the harbor defenses.

Because Anderson was sympathetic with the South although a Unionist, it was believed that he could satisfy the Carolinians while doing his duty to the United States. Floyd could not have been more conciliatory when he selected as ambassador in charge of the arsenal the most highly venerated South Carolinian in the United States Army and recipient of his state's Sword of Honor. If Ben Huger could not calm the people, no one could.

The ambassadors were anything but strangers to each other. They had gone through West Point together and were only a few months apart in age. An artillerist, Bob Anderson had often served during peacetime years on ordnance duty. The two had also served together in Mexico. During the Siege of Vera Cruz, Anderson had been in command of one of Huger's mortar batteries. While recovering from a wound received at the Battle of Molino del Rey, the artillerist had shared with his ordnance friend the comforts of a Mexican general's house during the occupation of Mexico City. When orders were received to proceed to Charleston, the two gray-haired majors were enjoying a friendship of nearly forty years.

Huger arrived in Charleston on 20 November and assumed command of the arsenal, staying with the family of his brother Cleland Kinloch Huger. The city was aglow with enthusiasm and excitement. A new governor would soon be elected, the South Carolina legislature would issue a call for a convention to withdraw the state from the Union, and commissioners would be sent to Washington to negotiate for the public property. Other southern states were expected to join South Carolina in secession. Military companies were drilling day and night, and a prodigious South Carolina army was being created. It was generally believed by the people of the state that the position of commander in chief of the forces of the new republic would be offered to Huger.[4] When actually approached by leaders of the state on the matter of his resigning from United States service to take command of the state forces, Huger spoke of his obligation to the administration and presented a number of objections. He asked for time before committing himself to a final decision.

The atmosphere in Charleston was one of chronic ferocity where every false report spread like a blaze. Eight days after his arrival, Huger went out to Fort Moultrie on Sullivan's Island to consult with Anderson. There was the greatest excitement in the city, he said, on account of a rumor that four companies of regulars were coming on the *James Adger* to strengthen the Federal garrison; and the extremists were in favor of taking steamers to intercept the *Adger*. Was it true? Anderson told him that he had no intelligence of anything of the kind.[5]

There was talk everywhere throughout the state of the approaching battle of Fort Moultrie, and the mob in Charleston could scarcely be restrained from making an immediate assault. The fire-eaters were once kept back when Huger threatened that, if Moultrie were mobbed, he would fight by the side of his friend Anderson.[6]

Engineer Foster believed that the Unionist workmen he had sent to Fort Sumter and Castle Pinckney should be armed for defense against assault. For this reason, he called at the arsenal to ask Huger for a hundred muskets to divide among the loyal laborers. Huger said that he could not issue the muskets without special permission from Washington, not even for the short time required for the completion of the work on the two defenses. The citizens were excited enough by the repair and construction at these points—so much so that Huger once voiced the wish of seeing all the engineering work stopped and the appropriation returned to the Treasury. How would the fanatics react on learning the laborers loyal to the Union were armed?[7]

When Captain Foster wrote to Washington for permission to arm his workmen, his application was laid before War Secretary Floyd and endorsed, "Action deferred for the present." Foster soon retracted his request on learning that the workmen at Fort Sumter, the key position in the harbor, were disinclined to use force against either an armed mob or an attack by the state militia. Those employed at Castle Pinckney might prove more reliable, Foster wrote: "But the feeling here in regard to secession is become so strong that almost all are entirely influenced by it. I therefore judge it best to suspend all idea of arming them at present."[8]

Previously, Anderson, faced with a weak garrison and a poor defensive position, dispatched a report on 23 November for Floyd, in which he repeatedly urged the sending of reinforcements and advised the military occupation of Castle Pinckney and Fort Sumter to deter the citizens from attempting to take Moultrie. He was answered that information thought to be reliable indicated that no attack would be made on his command. He was to do nothing that might initiate an assault; but if attacked, he was expected to defend all under his authority to the best of his ability. Judging by the excitement produced by the *James Adger* alarm, the secretary believed that actual reinforcement would increase the excitement and lead to serious results. Help therefore would not be sent. On the same day that Floyd's answer was written, 1 December, Anderson again pressed the need for aid and asked to be instructed as to whether the forts were to be surrendered, and if not, what course he should pursue. The administration in Washington seemed unaware of the actual danger, but Anderson knew that Huger could possibly help.

Pikesville Arsenal's commanding officer had not been chosen for ambassadorial work alone. The secretary of war and the general-in-chief were equally desirous of obtaining his knowledge and advice on the situation in Charleston. They had recognized the need for a man who could counsel on military matters without allowing politics to enter, and Floyd had recently requested Huger to confer with Anderson on the state of affairs. Huger was then to proceed to the War Department as soon as he could safely leave his post.

On 5 December, Huger was joined by Anderson, who had come to the city for the purpose of conferring with him. Apparently to insure the accuracy of their appraisal of the situation, the ambassadors visited the mayor and several other prominent citizens. These Charlestonians seemed determined to do all in their power to prevent a mob attack, but they were equally determined that the harbor defenses must be theirs after secession. The next day Anderson confessed to the War Department that Huger was "more hopeful of a settlement of impending difficulties without bloodshed than I am."[9]

Huger left Charleston for Washington on the night of the seventh. Puzzled by and fearful of his sudden absence, South Carolina's Governor States Rights Gist wired Cleland Huger: "It is reported that your brother Ben has been recalled[;] doubt, distrust & anxiety are hourly on the increase." Like his brother, Cle was anxious to reduce the excitement with a view to peace. He answered that Ben had gone merely to join his family, stopping to see the secretary of war on his way, but would return if wanted.[10]

When Huger reported to Floyd, he lent support to the sound advice previously given by Anderson. He had visited Fort Moultrie during the past week, he said, and had found that the garrison consisted of two companies of some sixty men present for duty. He told the secretary that, if the object was to guard the public property there from any unauthorized or lawless attack, this force was sufficient. But if it was intended to hold Moultrie against the demand of the state government, he went on, the force was entirely too small. He insisted that, in case of actual hostilities, as forces from several other southern states would no doubt be combined against the garrison, it would be necessary to defend the forts of the harbor with an army, supported and provisioned by a fleet. Therefore he thought it due Major Anderson that he be definitely instructed what to do in case their possession was demanded by the state authority. Huger explained that it was not his place to determine the policy of the government, but he did not see the use of attempting the defense of one or more of the forts at that point with an entirely insufficient force when the first blow would cause all the vacant forts at other points to be seized by the southerners. Floyd himself was against reinforcement because he felt it would mean certain war; but he asked Huger to express his views in a letter to General Scott, who was then at his headquarters in New York City. Not long after Huger committed the facts to paper, word arrived that the general-in-chief was coming to Washington.[11]

Huger conversed with Scott on 14 December. Scott concurred with the ambassador's views and next day urged the president to reinforce Anderson. Buchanan believed that there was no danger of early secession except in South Carolina. He replied that, when the commissioners from the state would arrive, he and Congress would negotiate with them. Should Congress decide against the secession, he would then send reinforcements, not before.

A problem arose at the Charleston Arsenal during Huger's absence. On the seventeenth, Foster went to the arsenal to obtain muskets for the two ordnance sergeants at Fort Sumter and Castle Pinckney. The sergeants had applied to him for arms, to which they were entitled; and Huger had directed that the muskets be delivered to Foster. When Foster asked Humphreys for the muskets and accouterments, the arsenal commander replied that he had no authority to issue two muskets for that purpose. There was no written proof of Huger's authorization, but there was an old order on file to issue forty muskets and accouterments to the engineer. The requisition had been approved by Floyd on 31 October, and an order had accordingly been issued by the ordnance department on the first of November. At the same time, the commandant at Moultrie had objected to receiving the arms, believing that acceptance would give the appearance of arming the workmen. That officer had been removed; and Anderson, his successor, wanted arms. These muskets were already packed and awaiting delivery. Foster received them, and after issuing arms to the ordnance sergeants, placed the remainder in the magazines of the two forts.

The twenty-man state guard was still in close surveillance at the arsenal. Word of the removal of the arms passed to Major General John Schnierle, commander of the state militia in that vicinity. The general called on Humphreys the next morning to warn him that a violent demonstration was certain unless the excitement could be allayed, adding that Huger had assured the governor that no arms would be removed from the arsenal. As the order by which the issue had been made was dated prior to Huger's visit in Charleston, Humphreys felt himself placed in a peculiar position from having acted contrary to the ambassador's assurance. He pledged his word therefore that the forty muskets would be returned the following night and addressed a request to Foster. Foster replied that he could not comply with the request because compliance would place the lives of his officers, his workmen, the two ordnance sergeants, and the government property in his charge at the mercy of a mob; but he was willing to refer the matter to Washington.

Foster met with Humphreys and Schnierle on the nineteenth. He found that the general's action of the day before had arisen from a great desire to eliminate the excitement among some of the citizens. Foster presumed that Huger must have acted by the authority of the government in giving his assurance to Governor Gist. But as neither Foster himself nor Humphreys had been informed by Huger that such assurance had been given and in the absence of any positive written testimony of the fact, Foster telegraphed to the ordnance office in Washington to inquire if the muskets should be returned.

Another wire was dispatched to Washington late at night, this one from an angry Charlestonian. The recipient of the telegram was Assistant Secretary of State William Henry Trescot, a native of Charleston. He thought the message announcing the removal of arms important enough to take it to Floyd's lodging immediately. Foster received a peremptory telegram from the war secretary at 2 A.M. to return the arms instantly. The resentful engineer officer informed the head of his corps, "The defense [of Sumter and Pinckney] now can only extend to keeping the gates closed and shutters fastened, and must cease when these are forced."[12]

Meanwhile, South Carolina's secession convention, which had fled from an incipient smallpox epidemic in Columbia, reconvened in Charleston on the eighteenth in a violently secessionist mood. An Ordinance of Secession was unanimously adopted two days later which proclaimed that the union between South Carolina and the other states was dissolved. Citizens, hotheads, and fanatics rejoiced. Governor Francis W. Pickens, who had taken office on the sixteenth, suddenly became the head of the sovereign Republic of South Carolina and selected a cabinet, or executive council as it was called. The state convention had resolved to send three commissioners to Washington to inform the government there of the state's independence and to persuade that foreign power to purchase peace by relinquishing possession of the Charleston forts and other public property. The commissioners began their two-day train ride on Christmas Eve.

Huger, who had left Washington for Pikesville on the fifteenth, ending his diplomatic mission, was quietly following events in the newspapers. A telegraphic dispatch from his

brother Cleland arrived: "The governor requests me to say
that[,] if you mean to resign now[,] he thinks the time [should
be] before our commissioners reach Washington[. C]ome on as
soon as you can[. Even] if you wont take office[,] he wants your
advice above all others[.]"[13]

On the same day, Christmas Eve, Huger answered the
telegram in a letter to his seventy-two-year-old cousin Alfred
Huger, Charleston's postmaster for nearly a generation. Before
secession, Alfred had volunteered his assistance to the state
convention and the governor and was now working closely with
Pickens.[14] In his communication to the governor through his
cousin, Huger explained that the administration desired peace
and all the influence available to assist that body in promoting
tranquility. His long service and connection in the army, he
felt, made him bound to the administration. Clearly, if he accepted command of the South Carolina army or went to
Charleston as an advisor, which basically amounted to the
former choice, the exercise of either position would cause the
kind of undue excitement the administration was trying to
eliminate. If the national government were to be dissolved, it
would be by public opinion, he asserted, in which case the
people would no doubt be in favor of a peaceful, conservative,
and permanent reorganization of the country. He would join
his state at the time of that reorganization. If he accepted command of the army at the present time, he pointed out, he would
be placing himself in a political position as well as a military
one. He was a soldier and nothing else. He admitted that, while
occupying such a position, his own desire for peace would affect
his judgment and might cause the state harm. "I must
[therefore] decline an appointment from the present Govt of
the State," his letter concluded.[15]

The inquiry, demand, and expectation in South Carolina
regarding Huger's service there had swelled to fanatical pro-
portion since his departure from Charleston. On Christmas
Day, before his letter reached his cousin, Alfred was pressed to
inform him of the fact. Enclosing a copy of the secession ordinance, the governor's volunteer assistant wrote:

> The demand for *yourself* & *your services* is universal,
> from the convention to the Governor, and from the

Governor to the lowest among our people, who have
intelligence to *perceive*, or sensibility to *feel*. ... In a
word the clamour for you cannot be restrained & will not
be satisfied [without you]. So I urgently submit to you
the propriety of coming—and of coming without delay—
announcing by telegram that you are en route. I know
the difficulties and the objections[.] I respect them & ap-
preciate them, but they do not smother the public voice,
and do not reach an agitation on the subject, which
amounts to fanaticism. The Governor is reported to me
by a common friend to have said, "We cannot do
without Col. Huger. We want his 'service'[,] his 'history'
and his 'name'[''']—and afterwards added, "Even if he
refuses to resign & join us, he *must* come & give his
counsel & his influence." Such a requisition, made as it
is in the name of the state, as our mother, I would certainly have you come, tho' you postpone your final
decision. But that you can do more good than any other
man is certain.[16]

For a reason unaccountable at the time, the original letter
never reached Huger.

The administration in Washington, failing to understand the situation in Charleston, sent Anderson orders too
vague and contradictory for guidance. The commander of the
harbor defenses knew, as did the local citizens, that Fort
Moultrie was indefensible and in an exposed position, while
Fort Sumter, located at a strategic point near the entrance to
the harbor, was secure. Huger had advised Anderson to move
his garrison from Moultrie to Sumter.[17] Under cover of darkness on the twenty-sixth, Anderson accordingly executed the
move. The transfer was made on his own responsibility for the
preservation of peace and the protection of his men.

The move exploded a political bombshell over the land.
A delegation of South Carolina congressmen who had consulted with the president claimed that Buchanan had solemnly
pledged that the military status at Charleston would not be
altered. The Carolinians were quick to believe this gross exag-
geration. As commander of the coastal defenses, Anderson had
the right by law to transfer his garrison to any point within the

limits of his authority. But South Carolina was in massive revolution. The hotheads were accusing the president of having broken his pledge when Anderson had taken a position of "hostility." Heatedly, state forces took possession of Castle Pinckney, Forts Moultrie and Johnson, the customhouse and post office, and occupied the United States arsenal, Humphreys surrendering with his men. The fact that these seizures occurred while the Palmetto commissioners were in Washington to negotiate for the now stolen property enraged the North.

An irate president determined to send help to Anderson. The act was not aggression, Buchanan felt, because his plain duty was to try to keep possession of Fort Sumter, which had become the only visible token that the administration meant to oppose the revolution. The representatives from South Carolina, still in Washington, implored Pickens to prepare for war. The governor rushed to Fort Moultrie to spur preparations for defense. Ladies were set to work making bandages. The harbor lights were extinquished. A militia general made an immediate tour of inspection of the recently captured defenses. He reported on the condition of the forts and their garrisons in words of despair. Worse yet, it was soon reported that the armed revenue cutter *Harriet Lane*, with a shipment of regulars, was on its way to reinforce Anderson. Charleston was swept with panic.

Huger's letter declining the governor's offer was yet unknown in South Carolina, the mail being delayed by the holiday. Correspondence began to reach him. "See my letter. Telegraph me that you are coming," read a wire from Alfred Huger. Another telegram arrived from Charleston secessionist leader Robert N. Gourdin: "Where are you in our time of trouble? South Carolina needs the arm of every son for her defense[.]" A lengthy letter came from Alfred Ford Ravenel, the husband of Huger's deceased youngest sister and president of the Northeastern Railroad with headquarters in Charleston. Ravenel mentioned Alfred Huger's letter of 25 December and expressed the reactions toward Anderson's move to Sumter, enclosing an article on the subject from the bellicose *Mercury*, and emphasized, "Your friends have been deeply anxious as to your decision."[18]

The reaction in Charleston was profound indeed when

word was received from Huger that his cousin's letter of
Christmas Day had not reached him and his own letter to
Alfred of the day before was read on the twenty-ninth. It
therefore appeared that he was declining command without
being aware of the enormous demand for his service or realizing the state's unreadiness to meet armed opposition. After
sending a hasty telegram north, Ravenel began packing and
left for Washington on one of his trains the same night to meet
Huger at Willard's Hotel on Monday afternoon, the thirty-
first. Cleland Huger rushed to the telegraph office the next day
to dispatch an urgent appeal: "The governor & executive council[,] of which the President of [the secession] convention is
one[,] beg you for God['ls sake to come & advise with them at
once. Answer. To understand the danger[,] you must come
and see[.]"[19]

As requested, Huger appeared in Willard's, where he
met with Ravenel and was given a copy of Alfred Huger's
letter of the twenty-fifth. No doubt the South Carolina commissioners, senators, representatives, and other dignitaries
from the state united with Ravenel in the most forceful exer-
tions to inform him of the critical situation in Charleston and
to persuade him to take command of the provisional army immediately. Huger had hoped to see his state secede in a correct,
dignified, nonviolent manner; and this must have formed the
basis of the opposition he expressed. But how could the infant
republic maintain its sovereignty without repelling the invaders? How could he refuse to defend his native state in such
a crisis? Questions like these were doubtless asked of him. New
Year's Day 1861 passed in further discussion. Huger departed
Washington on 2 January with mixed thoughts. He had promised to reconsider.

On his return to Pikesville, Huger found an alarming
telegram from Trescot, who had left office when their state
separated from the Union. Floyd, a southerner opposed to violence, had threatened to resign instantly if the administration
undertook to use force. It was known that Postmaster General
Joseph Holt had urged the president to reinforce Anderson
earlier in the dispute. Trescot's wire read: "Holt is sec at war.
[T]hat means civil war. I think you ought to know it[.]"[20]

Time was as pressing for Huger's decision as was the threat to his home state. He had returned from a capital torn by dissention and pervaded by distrust and fear. Field artillery had been placed in the Capitol and Treasury buildings in anticipation of an invasion of Washington. Southerners were resigning continually. North and South were at each other's throats, and Huger was in the midst of it. Armed conflict seemed inevitable. If he declined this time, he might be abandoning his state to an unhappy destiny.

Personal considerations likewise demanded attention. Huger wanted to see a prosperous, independent South, free from northern domination. And what about his career? He had seen some of his friends to whom he had been senior as a captain in Mexico soar to colonels and general officers, while he was still at the rank and pay of a major. Now he was being offered a generalship and supreme command of an army— every soldier's dream.[21] But it was a politico-military position which would place him at the controlling center of the dispute, the spot which could trigger national slaughter. Like his friend Lafayette, he viewed an American civil war as the ultimate atrocity of suffering and ruin.

A telegram reached him at 31 Cathedral Street, his recently acquired Baltimore home, on 4 January. It was from Ravenel: "Determine I beseech you. Moments [are] precious to you & all of us. What I said falls far short of demand[,] enquiry[,] expectation. We are on the brink of conflict[. C]ome as our advisor if nothing else. Commissioners at home. Telegraph me something this very night if you can[.]"[22] Huger had given his final decision the day before as an answer to Alfred's letter of 25 December, and it was yet on its way to Charleston. In his latest letter, he commented that, in his previous communication to Alfred:

> I explained why I could not throw up my commission upon this administration & take other service without a due regard to what is just and decent.
>
> Your present letter states that there is a clamor for my services. Of course it is only as a military man that they are required. When we both wrote[,] there was no pros-

pect of any enemy, and I felt that I should render myself
no credit in spending the money and means of the State
in keeping up an undue excitement about an imaginary
enemy. Enemies you have[,] God knows, but they are to
be combatted by other means.

Since that time[,] affairs have changed by the conduct of
Major Anderson; but this was the act of an individual. He
alone took the responsibility for what he thought the *safety*
of his command, and now the whole State seems disposed
to make war upon him and his handful of men.

Recollect, Maj A. and myself went to West Point
together 40 years [ago] and have been comrades in the
Army from that day to this, & I am now to take service
& make war upon him & his sixty men!! Now as you say
I am asked 'to come and give my counsel & influence'.
My first counsel would be, not to attack or molest Maj^r.
Anderson's command. In such times of excitement, men
of sense should endeavor not to let *side issues* divert
them from the great result proposed; now in our case,
where the State is first in a movement dependent upon
the public opinion and sympathy of other [southern
states] for its success, the great element, to allow the
development of this public opinion, is *time*. To gain this
time, you want to keep every thing as quiet as possible,
& make delays if necessary. Such negotiations were[,]
I hoped[,] in progress, when this movement of Maj
Anderson's made a new issue, and under the excitement[,]
all hopes of adjustment are likely to be destroyed. I
should say, *allay* the excitement as much as possible. If
it is considered necessary to hold the Forts with a view
to keep others out, put as few men in them as possible,
and why station men and take military possession of the
Arsenal? A note to Capt Humphreys would accomplish
the object.

My counsel and influence would be given by all
honorable means to gain *time* and not to commit any act
tending to a civil war, which none of us may see the
end of.

Our *friends* here think violent action at this time is
giving aid to our fanatical enemies and tends to alienate

our friends.

I only wish my *influence* was sufficient to cause my *counsel* to prevail. God help us.[23]

While Huger's fellow Carolinians were seeking his leadership, he had been seeking wisdom. In so doing, he had given up a soldier's dream for the cause of peace. But he had lost more than a generalship and unique popularity in the South. Heavy batteries were being planted to surround Fort Sumter, and the governor knew of no officer of heavy ordnance more experienced than Huger. To the citizens, he had abandoned his state in its darkest hour. There was great ill-feeling toward him in Charleston even among his relations.[24]

The rumor that the *Harriet Lane* was approaching had, in fact, been false. But the unarmed merchant steamer *Star of the West*, with a cargo of provisions and reinforcements sent by the president, was indeed en route. Defense work continued with all haste, and intensive recruiting was to end with an army more than half the size of the United States force.

The *Star of the West* was fired on and repelled from Charleston harbor on 9 January. Pickens placed the highest value on the counsel of military men, and Huger's advice wielded top priority.[25] Instead of opening fire on Fort Sumter, he sent a polite request to Anderson to capitulate. Anderson had no authority to surrender the fort. He knew that time would allow an increase in the number of batteries that would oppose him but might also afford an opportunity for peaceful negotiation. He proposed that Pickens send a commissioner to Washington to present the demand while he would send one of his officers to report on the condition of the fort. Isaac W. Hayne, attorney general in the executive council, left for Washington as Pickens's commissioner, with Robert Gourdin as his assistant, accompanied by Anderson's quartermaster. Two United States Army majors had thus averted the opening of a civil war.

Hayne, who arrived in Washington on 13 January, called at the White House the next day. But Buchanan, who regarded secession as illegal, refused to conduct official intercourse with representatives of the so-called republic, declined to hold any conversation with Hayne, and insisted that everything be in writing.

Huger received notice from his cousin Alfred on the fourteenth that the representatives from Charleston were expected to arrive in Washington the same day. He immediately left for the capital. That night he was discussing with Hayne and Gourdin a subject which distressed him. After the Sumter move, mail destined for the garrison had been stopped by the angry governor. Huger was also disturbed by Anderson's inability to purchase provisions of fresh meat and vegetables from Charleston merchants since the time of the *Harriet Lane* scare. The diet on the island prison was almost exclusively limited to water and salt pork. Apparently Huger went so far as to solicit the support of the southern senators in his determination to end this abuse of Anderson's command. Then he applied to the Charleston postmaster:

> My object in writing to you at once is to request [that] you will ask for me from the proper authority that my old friend & comrade Maj Anderson & his command be treated with a courtesy not extended to him heretofore— And that he be allowed to receive his mails and to procure such supplies as are required. Maj A. has no authority to give up the Fort; and confining him to salt diet &c. will not make the authorities here more willing to do so; but uncivil treatment of him & his command does harm to your cause, among your own friends.
>
> I beg [that] this matter may be attended to at once, & I am sure [that] it will have a favorable effect in assisting the Gentlemen here [the commissioners] to accomplish what they desire.[26]

The power of Huger's influence on the governor was again felt. He was answered as fast as action could be initiated, "Your last from Washington came this morning—all restrictions as to Major Anderson have been removed . . ." Alfred added that Anderson was "a brave & honorable man" toward whom he could never have "other than feelings of respect & consideration . . . enhanced by the fact that Major A is your friend." In addition to restoring mail service to the Sumter garrison, Pickens went so far as to direct an officer to purchase and to convey to the fort each day with the mail such supplies from the city market as Anderson would indicate. Not awaiting an initial grocery list from Sumter's commander, the quartermaster general of the state sent by the mailboat two hundred pounds of red beef and bags of turnips, potatoes, and other delicacies. Anderson was dumbfounded. He had not represented a need for commissary supplies and had no idea that the sudden kindness and generosity had originated from his old friend at Pikesville. Bitter from many acts of harshness and incivility since his removal from Fort Moultrie, he chose not to accept any civility that could be considered as a favor or an act of charity. He politely declined the gift of provisions, requesting that he be permitted to buy sustenance in the customary way. Pickens consented to this, but the grocers seemed to have conspired not to sell to the garrison.[27]

The *Star of the West* incident induced other southern states to follow South Carolina's example in seceding from the Union. Most southern leaders shared Huger's opinion that Sumter should be secured by negotiation as opposed to bloodshed. They wanted a peaceful separation of their states and had plans for the creation of a central government. Pickens, a target of Charleston critics for allowing Anderson to receive mail and provisions, realized that the taking of Sumter would restore some measure of his popularity. But he also knew that he would be condemned by these leaders if he initiated war before the Confederacy was organized, and he was yet without a suitable army commander. Thus were his hands tied when Commissioners Hayne and Gourdin returned to Charleston, having been unsuccessful in their mission to purchase Sumter and the rest of the public property in the state.

The reaction above and below the Mason-Dixon line to Huger's course of action could be typified by two letters he received in February. One came from Major General Braxton Bragg, commander in chief of Lousiana's army. Bragg wrote: "We hoped you would be in command in South Carolina before this, as they sadly need a head, but hear with regret that you decline. Now that we are to have a consolidated government and regular forces, I hope your objections may be removed."

Brevet Major Peter V. Hagner, who had been Huger's second in command in Mexico and had recently refused a colonelcy to head Virginia's newly created ordnance department, wrote: "I can well feel[,] my dear Col.[,] how many influences have been brought upon you—far beyond [Virginia's efforts to gain my service]—to persuade you to hasty action . . . Knowing and feeling the good influence your delay has exerted, I have rejoiced in your course, and I still look with confidence to your future. May God bless you . . . "[28]

With the formation of the government of the Confederate States of America, the governor of the onetime Republic of South Carolina applied to President Jefferson Davis for someone qualified to fill the dusty vacancy of commander in chief of the Palmetto State army. Brigadier General P. T. G. Beauregard, holding the highest rank then authorized in the army the South was raising, arrived in Charleston on 3 March to take command of the disappointed Carolinians. He was not Huger, but he would have to do.[29]

The first of a trio of commissioners, this time from the new southern government, arrived in Washington in a last attempt to reach a settlement. When Lincoln delivered his Inaugural Address the next day, the fourth, he expressed the determination to maintain the property belonging to the Federal government and to continue to collect the duties imposed on the South, adding that no state could lawfully remove itself from the Union. The South entertained a different point of view: the states had entered the Union voluntarily and had the right to leave it voluntarily.

Believing that Sumter would be reinforced, Beauregard ordered the supply of food to the garrison discontinued. A day later, 8 April, a confidential messenger from Lincoln announced to Pickens that an attempt would be made to supply Sumter with provisions only and that, if no resistance were met, there would be no reinforcement of Anderson's command without further notice. The South now felt that it must capture the fort or confess a lack of sovereignty. On the twelfth, all the passions which had been rising in South Carolina since 1828 suddenly exploded into an actual bombardment of Fort Sumter. The time had come:

Washington   April 13, 1861

Sir,
    I request [that] the President will accept my
resignation of the commissions I have heretofore held
in the Army of the United States.
                    Very respectfully
                    Your obt. sert.
                    Benj. Huger
                    Bvt. Col. U.S.A.
                    Major of Ordnance.
Col: L Thomas,
    Adj Genl U.S. Army
    Washington.[30]

A quiet man who had done all he could for the preservation of peace, hoping against hope that the dispute could be
settled by some miracle at the conference table, Huger had
refused to despair until the very last hour. Both he and
Anderson had been swept up in a surge of events too powerful
for either of them to stop.

Confronted by the nightmare in Charleston, Huger felt
no more inclination to join the South against the North than to
fight with the North against the South. There was but one
alternative remaining. He would enter civilian life. Such was
his intention when he penned his resignation and composed an
accompanying letter:

                    Washington.   April 13, 1861

Lieut Genl Winfield Scott.

                    My dear General,
    I feel compelled by the course of events to request
the President to accept my resignation. I do not do
this for the purpose of taking service against any
portion of my countrymen. My object is, if possible, to
retire to private life. After thirty-six years['] con-
tinuous service in the Army, it is with extreme regret
[that] I feel compelled to part from it now; but unhappy
political divisions have resulted in civil war. I desire

to take no part in such fratricidal strife.
My comrades in service will bear me witness, and my
record will show, that[,] in the battles of our country[,]
I have not been backward in sustaining her flag.
I must be excused from warring on my Countrymen.
With much respect & esteem
Your friend & comrade
Benj. Huger[31]

The day after this letter was written, Anderson surrendered Sumter and was sent north with his command.

Maryland's sympathies were divided, and the activity of
the state militia was directed toward maintaining tranquility.
Rather than retreat from the problem facing a divided nation,
Huger tendered his service to Maryland, convinced that the
duty of a good citizen was to preserve order. Stationed at
historic Fort McHenry in Baltimore harbor (birthplace of the
National Anthem), he served as the commanding officer of the
Fifty-third Regiment, commonly known as the "Maryland
Guards of Baltimore." His cool and judicious counsel
prevented rash actions and enterprises which were projected
by some of the more indiscreet. On 10 May he placed the
Pikesville Arsenal in charge of its master armorer and soon
after resigned his militia commission.

Unlike most military men, his love of peace transcended
allegiance to the Union or loyalty to his native state.

3. An Exile in Virginia

Civil war had become a tragic reality, the North insistent on preserving the Union, the South seeking independence. Devotion to the cause of the South induced Huger to travel to Richmond and offer his service to Virginia in any capacity.[1] Joining his own state had been out of the question. Although a few state officials had realized the rare purity of thought which had dictated his course during the recent crisis—and had named him colonel of artillery on 16 March—most South Carolinians cruelly denounced him.[2]

The three points in Virginia considered as vital were Harpers Ferry, Norfolk, and the Yorktown Peninsula, between the James and York rivers. The Potomac post, under Colonel Thomas J. (later Stonewall) Jackson, could not be long defended. The Federal armory, which Huger had commanded seven years before, and the Harpers Ferry Arsenal had been damaged when the evacuating United States troops had set fire to the buildings; but the several thousand new small arms and the immensely valuable machinery for their manufacture had escaped the flames and were desperately needed by the state. The town would have to be held until all the weapons and equipment could be transported to Richmond. To Huger came the task of emplacing large guns as they arrived at London Heights (on the Virginia side of the Potomac), Maryland Heights, and Bolivar Heights.

In another corner of the state, Norfolk offered an incalculable advantage. Virginia was exceedingly vulnerable to attack by a power commanding the sea, yet the state possessed few naval vessels. The Gosport Navy Yard at Portsmouth afforded the best if not the only opportunity for the construction and repair of warships in any short time. Possession of the Norfolk area, which guarded Portsmouth, would enable the South to offset the superior northern navy.

When Huger arrived in Richmond to procure whatever might be necessary for the efficiency of the heavy batteries at Harpers Ferry, he was welcomed by the recently named commander in chief of the army and navy of Virginia, his junior in Mexico. Major General Robert E. Lee had recently spent two or three days inspecting Norfolk. There had been some hints that the commanding officer there, Brigadier General Walter Gwynn, who had not seen regular military service since 1832, was submerged in detail. Lee had found an atmosphere of excitement and confusion. He had seen that progress on the fortifications was slow. Aside from sharing a long personal friendship, Lee regarded Huger as "an officer of great merit" and placed full confidence in him. Having determined to relieve Gwynn, he asked Huger to take command of the state forces at Norfolk and its vicinity. Virginia endorsed Lee's confidence in Huger when the state convention, on 22 May, appointed him a brigadier general of volunteers.

Gwynn meanwhile, hearing that he was to be relieved of command, telegraphed his resignation to Governor John Letcher on the twenty-third. At 10 o'clock that night, Huger's orders from Lee were written hastily in a note: "You will soon see what is to be done & will know how to do it. Put all things to rights & keep every body hard at work. We have not an hour to lose. Rely upon yourself for creating what you want." Arriving at his new station on the twenty-fifth, Brigadier General Huger moved into the customhouse, the headquarters of what was soon to be designated the Department of Norfolk.[3]

To resist invasion, endangered areas of the Confederacy were divided into geographical military departments. When invasion came, department commanders were to borrow or lend one another troops and supplies. Huger's departmental boundaries were the James River and Hampton Roads (the largest natural harbor in the world) on the north, the Blackwater and Chowan rivers on the west, the Atlantic Ocean on the east, and Albemarle Sound, North Carolina, on the south. Federal authority had been overthrown everywhere in Virginia except at Huger's old post opposite Norfolk, Fort Monroe, which had been too powerful for the state's volunteers to assault. If the enemy ascended the Nansemond River and seized Suffolk, a land force could be sent against Norfolk by rail from that direction. Clearly, Norfolk would have to be guarded from a turning movement by way of Suffolk as well as from direct attack.

Huger applied himself with skill and industry to the completion of the defenses of his position. Under his direction, the construction and arming of the batteries proceeded with less delay. He expertly protected Norfolk on land with eighty-five heavy guns placed in six batteries to cover the Elizabeth River and secured the mouth of the river with powerful batteries on Craney Island and Sewell's Point. He also obstructed the channel between Sewell's Point and Willoughby's Point. To prevent an enemy ascent of the Nansemond and occupation of the railroads west of Norfolk, three batteries mounting nineteen guns were constructed along the shores of that river, the battery at Pig Point covering its mouth. The armament and command of the batteries along the two rivers had been assigned to officers of the Virginia navy, they being the most experienced artillerists. In addition to the batteries, elaborate field works were constructed, in many instances exceeding those of the batteries. Huger displayed marked ability and organized a fine department.

Virginia's army was transferred to the Confederate States on 8 June and the naval forces two days later. Lee would serve for a time as commander of the coastal defenses of South Carolina, Georgia, and East Florida and then as military advisor to President Davis, being promoted to full general in the regular army of the Confederacy at the end of August to rank from June. Huger was named brigadier general in the provisional army on 17 June and major general on 7 October. With the position of commander in chief of Virginia's army no longer existent, the Department of Norfolk became a semi-autonomous command; and Huger communicated directly with the secretary of war, the secretary of the navy, and the president.

Being in close proximity to Union Major General John E. Wool's Department of Virginia at Fort Monroe, Norfolk was designated an exchange point for prisoners of war and for civilians going North or South. Incalculable numbers of prisoners were exchanged according to the cartel agreed on between the United States and Great Britain during the War of 1812.

On the peninsula just above Wool's garrison of twelve thousand men was Huger's "old army" friend Major General John B. Magruder. The Virginian was in command of the Department of the Peninsula with headquarters at historic Yorktown. The "Prince of Humbug," as Huger called him, was a perfectionist in drama and master of deception. Delightfully peculiar, "Prince John" always ate from a gold plate using gold eating utensils.

After the Battle of Manassas on 21 July, Major General George B. McClellan was appointed to command the demoralized Union Army of the Potomac, and for a time, succeeded Scott as general-in-chief. He organized his army into an efficient combat force of over one hundred thousand men—the largest army ever commanded by one person in the history of the Western Hemisphere. By early December, he developed a plan aimed at capturing the Confederate capital at Richmond by transporting his army down the Potomac River and the Chesapeake Bay to the tip of the Virginia Peninsula. Then sending his supply ships up the York River, he intended to march up the peninsula, join Major General Irvin McDowell's Department of the Rappahannock, originally his First Corps, which would be marching overland from Washington, and together, converge on Richmond.

In the early months of the war, Brigadier General Ambrose E. Burnside held a training command in Washington, where his task was to train and equip the new regiments before sending them on to join the Army of the Potomac. When it was decided to organize a division for coastal service in the bays and inlets of the Potomac and Chesapeake, McClellan late in October assigned the task of organizing the amphibious command to Burnside. As McClellan's plan to take Richmond matured, Burnside recruited and trained New Englanders experienced in boating and working around the water to prepare for an expedition which was soon destined to leave the Potomac.

Earlier, in late August, on hearing of the capture of Hatteras Inlet on the North Carolina coast, Huger sent a regiment to occupy Roanoke Island, some forty-five miles north of Hatteras, and to erect fortifications on the island as promptly as possible. As the island was outside the limits of his geographical department, he ordered its occupation on his own responsibility, in order to prevent the enemy from passing into Albemarle Sound. If the Federals gained possession of the sound, they could take advantage of the numerous rivers, canals, and railroads in the area to invade northeastern Carolina. Hence, Roanoke Island was the key to all the southern defenses of Norfolk. Furthermore, the island guarded more than four-fifths of all of Norfolk's supplies of corn, pork, and forage from the surrounding country and all of its most efficient transportation. Should the Confederates attempt the recapture of Hatteras, the island would be the proper place from which to begin the operation.

In September, Roanoke Island became part of a new military district in the Department of North Carolina. Huger's regiment was then withdrawn and returned to the Department of Norfolk. In December, Brigadier General Henry A. Wise took command of the district and was attached to Huger's department.

It was the misfortune of the Confederacy to give positions in the army to distinguished politicians. A recent governor of Virginia, General Wise possessed no more experience or ability in military command than Huger cared to have in politics. According to the sworn testimony of one of his officers, Wise was complaining with superiors, faultfinding with equals, insolent with subordinates, and opinionated in the superlative degree. He had raised a legion of infantry, cavalry, and artillery in western Virginia, where his blunders in the subsequent campaign there had damaged the reputation of his commander, General Lee.[4] The administration, having promptly relieved Wise of command in that theater, now pushed him on Huger.

It was known to the Confederates in early January 1862 that Burnside's expedition was headed south from Hampton Roads to strike at some point on the North Carolina coast. When Wise arrived at Roanoke Island, he conducted a thorough inspection of his new post. Probably owing to the fact that the command of the island had been frequently transferred from one officer to another, the fortifications had been seriously neglected and their positions badly selected. The defenses consisted of three turfed sand forts—Huger, Blanchard, and Bartow—located on the west side near the northern end and facing Croatan Sound, with a battery on the east side facing Roanoke Sound. Fort Forrest was located on the North Carolina side of the mainland nearly opposite Fort Huger. Wise noted that the fortifications should have been situated at the southern end of the island; for if the Burnside expedition were to strike that area of the coast, the approach would be from the south. On completion of his tour of inspection, Wise wrote to Huger for powder and reinforcements. Huger sent what powder he could but noted, "I think you want supplies, hard work, and coolness among the troops you have, instead of more men."[5]

Not satisfied with this, Wise went to Norfolk to protest in person. He again emphasized a need for more troops. He also stressed the necessity of making the defenses at the south end of the island, and Huger adopted the proposition of establishing batteries on the marshes there. At the end of the discussion, Wise left a memorandum of the necessary requisitions for supplies and materiel. In orders to Wise written that day, 13 January, Huger approved the requisitions but rejected Wise's suggestion of reinforcing the district with additional troops. Commenting on the orders later that day, Wise claimed that "At least 3,000 infantry are needed on the island, and a considerable force, say 1,500 more, are needed on the beaches, and if the enemy pass Roanoke, 5,000 at least are necessary to fight them on the tongues of land on the north side of Albemarle Sound."[6]

Violating military law, Wise went without orders a few days after his meeting with Huger to confer with the authorities in Richmond. He was allowed but a brief and cursory consultation with Secretary of War Judah P. Benjamin, during which he urged that the whole force of his legion be forwarded to him at once, along with reinforcements. To the appeal for reinforcements, the secretary replied that he had no men to spare. Wise stated that Huger had fifteen thousand idle troops defending the front of Norfolk and that a considerable portion of them could be spared for the defense of the rear, especially in view of the fact that reinforcements at Roanoke Island were as necessary to the defense of Norfolk as were forces in its front. But Benjamin relied on Huger's professionalism rather than the opinion of a citizen-soldier, whom he had recently relieved in western Virginia. Failing to obtain any definite reply to his appeal, Wise remained in the capital from the nineteenth to the twenty-second of January engaged in urging the forwarding of his legion. On the twenty-third, having received from Benjamin an order to return to his post, he reached his headquarters on the mainland at Nags Head on the thirtieth. He was seized with an attack of pleurisy on 1 February but continued to dictate orders from his bed.

On the seventh, Burnside's armada passed into Croatan Sound with a supporting naval force under Commodore Lewis M. Goldsborough. While Goldsborough's warships bombarded the Confederate forts and gunboats, Burnside's troops landed unopposed near Ashby's Harbor. The next day the Federals defeated Wise's estimated four thousand men and took some three thousand prisoners. Among the Confederate dead was Captain O. Jennings Wise, the general's son.

Burnside's success coincided with the capture of Forts Henry and Donelson in Tennessee and did much to depress the morale of the South. The defeat also afforded the enemy material advantages. A strong blockade was established along the Atlantic coast of the Confederacy, and all but two of its ports were either occupied or sealed off by Federal forces. On the tenth, a group of Goldsborough's gunboats in the Pasquotank River destroyed the small Confederate squadron. Having complete control of the waterways, Burnside spread his operations to the mainland. Winton and various points about Currituck Sound were taken. In the two months following, New Bern, Beaufort, Morehead City, North Carolina, and Elizabeth City were added to his successes. Expeditions from New Bern were sent to operate against Washington, Plymouth,

and Edenton, North Carolina, and to threaten Suffolk and
Norfolk.

It was not long before Huger learned the cause of the
Roanoke Island disaster. He wrote to the adjutant general the
day after the island fell: "I send you a copy of my instructions
to General Wise as soon as he reported to me, dated January
13. These orders have never been carried out." In those orders,
he had instructed Wise to "establish batteries at the marshes
off [the] south end of the island," specifying "this to be the
first work done." At the same time, he made known his reason
for being convinced that large reinforcements were unneces-
sary, "If the batteries can keep off gunboats and transports[,]
the infantry will have little opportunity to act." Prior to the
battle, Burnside's ships had been compelled to pass between
the marsh islands in single file—easy targets if batteries had
been stationed there. President Davis wrote after the battle,
"My anxiety for the construction of a work on the south end of
the island was freely expressed to General Wise, and its importance appears to have been even greater than I supposed . . ."
The guns of Forts Huger and Blanchard had not been engaged
because Burnside's fleet had not come within their range, leaving for defense on the island only Fort Bartow. There had been
a total of at least thirty-five heavy cannons on the island and
at Fort Forrest which Wise could have relocated to oppose an
approach from the south. Not one gun had been moved.[7]

Wise claimed that he had not had time to begin, much
less complete, the change of defense of the shore batteries to
the marshes. What he neglected to add was that he had wasted
most of his time in the administration of uniting his scattered
legion, which could have been handled by a competent staff
officer, and in traveling back and forth from Nags Head to
Norfolk and Richmond protesting the numerical weakness of
his force. The large volume of his correspondence would indicate
that his opinion from the very beginning was that the island
could be successfully defended only by meeting the enemy
with overwhelming numbers, and he regarded his opinion as
military law. Hence, through his own folly, he had insured that
success depended entirely on reinforcements. His disobedience
of orders, rejection of sound advice, and the resulting blunders
completely deranged all of Huger's plans; and on 16 February,

Huger insisted that the general be relieved and that the disorganized Wise Legion be removed from his department. This was the second time that Wise had been relieved for incompetence within a period of five months. Anticipating all criticism and no doubt believing himself guiltless, he immediately began preparing a lengthy report and demanding a court of inquiry. Having been granted a furlough, he left for Richmond, where he had so recently lived as governor. He was still an influential political figure and had many influential friends. Newspapers were soon blaming Huger and War Secretary Benjamin for failure to send all available troops to the island. The *Richmond Enquirer* and the *Raleigh Register* screamed for a vindication of Wise. At the same time, Wise was lobbying through Congress an investigating committee to whitewash him and censure his two superiors. He succeeded in this better than against the enemy. Among the most vocal of his friends in denouncing Huger were two fellow Virginians, Congressman Henry S. Foote and former congressman and newspaper publisher Roger A. Pryor. The verdict, which had already been anticipated in the press, appeared in the committee's report in late March. Wise, of course, was completely exonerated from all responsibility for the defeat, while the already unpopular Benjamin, since transferred to secretary of state, was officially denounced along with Huger.

During the investigation, Wise charged that Benjamin had failed to meet his requisitions for munitions. What Wise did not know was that Benjamin submitted to censure rather than reveal to the congressional committee the Confederacy's poverty and inability to supply the requisitions and thus run the risk that the fact would become known to spies in the city.[8] But the fact of the matter was that Wise had not been deficient in munitions. A quantity of powder had reached the island from Norfolk, and artillery ammunition had been conveyed to Fort Bartow during the battle from the inactive Fort Huger. Burnside's ordnance officer reported an abundance of ammunition, most of which had been destroyed when the island was taken. Wise had, in fact, needed nothing more than the usual supplies of a district command, combined with "hard work," as Huger had advised a month before the battle.[9]

While the former governor was busily engaged in condemning the innocent, Huger was endeavoring to defend his position in spite of the blunders of his inept subordinate. After the fall of Roanoke Island, he received reports that thousands of McClellan's troops were landing at Fort Monroe and Newport News and that Burnside was being reinforced. With the enemy thus threatening both the front and rear of Norfolk, he sent troops to guard the railroads, to occupy Suffolk and South Mills as well as other important points, to cover the southern approaches to Norfolk, and to protect the defenses at Sewell's Point from a possible enemy landing in the area of Ocean View. He also obstructed the Elizabeth and Nansemond rivers. He established a large, ever-active signal company with posts extending at intervals from a station on the roof of his headquarters in Norfolk to Fort Huger on Harden's Bluff, by the south side of the James.

The principal objects to a front attack against Norfolk were the batteries at Sewell's Point and Craney Island. The enemy could land at different points to the south of the city, but from any point of landing, would have to march from thirty to fifty miles before reaching any vitally important point in Huger's department. Should the enemy approach from the rear, it was Huger's plan to launch a counteroffensive by vigorously attacking, and if possible, destroying the enemy while on the march. The vast country in his charge and the many rivers cutting through it presented impediments to a rapid concentration of troops within his department. When reinforcements were requested, they were sent to him immediately. Since it was not known to the Confederates whether McClellan intended to capture Richmond by way of Norfolk or the peninsula, Magruder was instructed to send all the forces he could spare across the James and cooperate with Huger; and Huger received similar instructions to cooperate with Magruder should the real attack be made against Yorktown. On 27 February, Norfolk and Portsmouth, the first cities in the Confederacy to be proclaimed in danger of attack, were placed under martial law.[10] The secretary of war assured Huger: "We are using every effort to strengthen your command. It seems evident that a great effort is to be made to capture Norfolk, and its defense must be as vigorous as the whole power of the Confederacy can make it."[11] A similar letter had been received from the president: "You will accept assurances of my readiness to sustain you to the full extent of my power . . ."[12]

But in Norfolk, a powerful new weapon would greatly reduce the threat to the city. The *U.S.S. Merrimack* had been captured by the Confederates early in the war among other vessels abandoned by Federal troops in the navy yard. The Confederates had raised it and had improvised an ironclad ram, renamed the *C.S.S. Virginia.* The armament of the ironclad consisted of ten heavy guns. Constructed for harbor defense, the *Virginia,* under Captain Franklin Buchanan, was completed on 5 March, and three days later, steamed into Hampton Roads with two small gunboats to attack the Federal ships there.

Gulls swooped over the surface of the roads, their shrill cries drowned by soldiers cheering wildly as the *Virginia* passed Confederate forts and batteries. Spectators, steadily increasing in number, lined the shores in every direction. The *Virginia* soon engaged the fifty-gun *Congress,* mutilating the wooden ship and its crew, while shells ricocheted harmlessly off its armor. Then it twice rammed the twenty-four-gun *Cumberland,* which sunk in a short time. The ironclad then turned its attention back to the *Congress,* which had meanwhile steamed toward shore and grounded. In moving into position, the *Virginia* passed heavily active shore batteries with impunity and silenced several of the guns. A large transport steamer was blown up, a schooner sunk, and another captured and sent to Norfolk. It poured a destructive fire of shot and shell at the *Congress* until the ship surrendered. The *Congress* was then set on fire and later exploded. Federal infantry fired from shore in support of their ships; and Buchanan, after being wounded in the thigh, turned the command of the *Virginia* over to his executive officer.

During the action, the batteries at Sewell's Point fired at the steam frigates *Minnesota, Roanoke,* and *Saint Lawrence,* which had been sent from Old Point Comfort to assist the *Congress* and *Cumberland.* The warships steered along the far edge of the channel to avoid the danger and ran aground before reaching their destination. The *Roanoke* was struck several times, and with the *Saint Lawrence,* returned to Old Point, leaving Goldsborough's flagship, the *Minnesota,* on a small shoal off Newport News. The *Virginia* retired to its anchorage behind Craney Island with the intention of returning the next day to destroy the *Minnesota*.

When the *Virginia* returned to Hampton Roads on 9 March, it found the Federal ironclad *Monitor* lying in advance of the *Minnesota*. A two-hour battle began between the ironclads, neither one inflicting significant damage on the other, though the *Monitor* was able to outmaneuver its rival. Not long after the *Virginia* concentrated its fire at the little pilothouse of the *Monitor*, a shell struck the sight hole and blinded the captain. The *Virginia* waited a short time after the *Monitor* withdrew and then moved triumphantly up the Elizabeth River toward drydock at Norfolk for repairs. Wooden warships had become obsolete. History's first battle between ironclad ships had ended and a new era of naval warfare begun.

On 2 April, McClellan arrived at Fort Monroe with the intention of commencing a multipronged thrust on the fourth to seize Yorktown and Norfolk. His advance up the peninsula was halted on the fifth, however, when it came unexpectedly against Magruder's defensive position. The "Prince of Humbug" so dazzled him with stunts to make his small command appear enormous that the Federal commander cautiously laid siege. This delayed him a month and served to fully reveal to Confederate authorities his plan to advance by way of the peninsula. The delay also provided sufficient time for General Joseph E. Johnston's Army of the Potomac to be withdrawn from Manassas and brought to meet McClellan's force. McClellan had expected McDowell's command at Fredericksburg to move so as to threaten Magruder's rear, but Lincoln was unwilling to leave Washington exposed by the removal of McDowell's forty thousand men. Joining Magruder, Johnston assumed command of the combined forces on the peninsula and of the Department of Norfolk.

Captain Josiah Tattnall had been appointed to replace the disabled Buchanan in command of the *Virginia* and its little squadron of gunboats. The ironclad, operating about Sewell's Point and Craney Island, kept McClellan and Wool at bay and prevented Goldsborough's fleet from protecting McClellan's transports for a movement up the James River toward Richmond.

On the nineteenth, a force from Burnside's expedition landed at Elizabeth City and marched toward South Mills, a hamlet in North Carolina where the Dismal Swamp Canal opened into the Pasquotank River. Its mission was to destroy the canal locks to prevent Confederate ironclads from passing into Albemarle Sound and to fortify and reinforce the position at South Mills with the view of threatening Norfolk in the rear while McClellan attacked the city in front. The Federals were defeated by one of Huger's regiments and retreated to their transports. Reinforced during the week, the enemy remained afloat near Elizabeth City and could land there again or anywhere along the Chowan River.

Troops had been sent from Magruder to reinforce the position at South Mills but had been returned to the peninsula before the engagement, and Brigadier General Raleigh E. Colston's brigade of Huger's department earlier in the month had been sent to Magruder. Huger's command was too weak to be scattered, and a superior force of the enemy could easily land and close in on Norfolk. When Johnston decided to withdraw his army up the peninsula, it was considered that Norfolk would be left untenable. Johnston sent orders to Huger on 27 April to be prepared to abandon Norfolk and move his troops toward Richmond.

On 2 May, Secretary of War George W. Randolph and Secretary of the Navy Stephen R. Mallory arrived in Norfolk to make preparations for the evacuation of the place and to save such machinery, stores, munitions, and arms as could be removed. A few hours after their arrival, an officer from Johnston made his appearance with an order for Huger to evacuate immediately. As obedience to the order would have involved heavy losses in public property, Secretary Randolph took the responsibility of giving Huger a written order to delay the evacuation until as much property as possible could be sent off. At the same time, Secretary Mallory gave similar instructions to Captain Sidney Smith Lee (brother of General Lee), commandant of the navy yard.

With the view of covering his withdrawal, Huger concentrated his troops near Suffolk to serve at the defenses on the southern shore of the James and to guard the approaches to Norfolk on the North Carolina side. He left in position only his signal corps and enough men to preserve order and prevent disloyal citizens from communicating with the enemy. The *Virginia* was to afford protection to the city and to hold Hampton Roads, thereby covering the escape to Richmond of the ironclad *Richmond* and other partially completed gunboats and the naval property being carried off by a Confederate flotilla.

Prompted by public impatience over the stalemate at Hampton Roads, President Lincoln, accompanied by Secretary of War Edwin M. Stanton and Secretary of the Treasury Salmon P. Chase, arrived at Fort Monroe on the evening of the sixth. Though unaware of the contemplated evacuation of Norfolk and the machinery trouble then plaguing the *Virginia*, he boldly ordered war vessels to harass Confederate ships on the James and directed Wool to capture Norfolk. He was soon informed by a southern traitor of the intended evacuation by the Confederates. Accordingly, on the morning of the eighth, he went to the *Monitor*, and in preparation of an amphibious landing near Norfolk, directed the commanding officer to proceed on a reconnaissance of the batteries at Sewell's Point to learn if the works had been abandoned or reinforced. This was perhaps the only time that a president of the United States gave an order in person for a tactical movement on the field of battle. He was then within easy range of shells from the point.

Six warships, the *Monitor* well in advance of the others, moved across the roads and began shelling the Sewell's Point batteries. The batteries flamed in reply. The firing continued into the early afternoon, when that of the batteries slackened and the flag over them was shot away. As a dense smoke rose above the trees on the point and moved toward the roads from the direction of Norfolk, the *Monitor* went back toward the rest of the gunboats. The smoke announced the arrival of the *Virginia*. The ironclad rounded the point, and the Federal gunboats ceased fire. As it approached them, they steamed away from it in an attempt to draw it into deep water where it might be rammed by high-speed steamers. The *Virginia*, however, returned to its usual anchorage at the point. No troops were landed on account of its presence.

High ranking officers of the Confederate army and navy

had planned to hold a conference that morning on the final disposition of the *Virginia*. Before the officers could assemble, however, the shelling of Sewell's Point began; and Flag Officer Tattnall had proceeded to the scene in the ironclad. Consequently, the conference was held on the ninth. Too unwell to attend, Huger sent his chief of staff and a second officer to represent him. It was supposed that the removal of public property would occupy a week or more. The officers agreed unanimously that the *Virginia* should continue to protect Norfolk in order to afford time for the removal of the property, to cover the withdrawal of Huger's remaining force, and to prevent the enemy's ascent of the James. Because of his position and rank, Huger exercised direct control over that portion of the navy within the geographical boundaries of his command. By previous arrangement, he would notify Tattnall when his preparations for evacuation were sufficiently advanced to enable the naval officer to act independently.

Unfortunately for the Confederates, Lincoln was a reflection of northern impatience. He ordered a landing at Willoughby's Point, some seven miles north of Norfolk. In the early morning darkness of the tenth, General Wool, accompanied by Secretary Chase, landed with a force of five thousand men and began marching toward Norfolk about 10 o'clock. When some five miles from the point of landing, the column encountered a Confederate battery on the other side of a bridge over a creek. The Confederates fired a few rounds into Wool's advance guard and then burned the bridge. This made the Federals march around five miles farther.

Huger received notice of the enemy's landing when the event occurred. He immediately sent an orderly to Captain Lee with a message to the effect that a large body of troops had landed, that he did not have a force sufficient to receive the enemy, and that the remaining military and naval personnel must evacuate at once.[13] His skeleton garrison had been collected at 4 A.M. and had left Norfolk by train. The unarmed men of his signal corps, the last of his command to depart, abandoned their posts about 7 P.M.

For an unknown reason, Huger's message did not pass from Lee to Tattnall. The first intimation of the complete evacuation of the Confederates presented itself to Tattnall at

10 A.M., when he observed from the *Virginia* that no flag was flying over the Sewell's Point batteries and that the works appeared to have been abandoned. Puzzled because the evacuation was supposed to be protracted at least another week and that Huger was to notify him when he could act independently, he sent his flag lieutenant to Craney Island, where the colors were still visible. When the lieutenant returned, he reported that the enemy was marching rapidly toward Norfolk. Tattnall then sent the lieutenant to Norfolk to confer with Huger and Lee. The lieutenant found the navy yard in flames and discovered that all its officers had left by railroad. Continuing, he found that Huger and all the other army officers had left also, that the enemy was within half a mile from the city, and that the mayor was treating for its surrender. As he returned to the ironclad, he found that all the batteries along the James had been abandoned. He arrived with the unexpected information at 7 o'clock in the evening.

The *Virginia* not being in a condition for battle, Tattnall determined to save the crew by landing the men at Craney Island, the only remaining route of escape, and to destroy the ship to prevent its capture. The ironclad was accordingly put on shore as near the mainland in the vicinity of the island as possible, and the crew landed. It was then set ablaze, and after burning fiercely for nearly an hour, exploded early on the morning of the eleventh.

That day was a jubilant occasion to Lincoln, Stanton, Chase, and Goldsborough as they toured the captured city together. Earlier, Goldsborough's fleet had entered Hampton Roads for the first time since 8 March, the *Monitor* having been the first of the fleet to steam into Norfolk. The fall of that city and the destruction of the *Virginia* allowed McClellan to change his line of supply from the York River to the James, which was now open to a point seven miles below Richmond. Gunboats were on the way to shell the Confederate capital into surrender.

Meanwhile, Confederate authorities feared the probability of a forward movement on the south side of the James by a combination of forces from McClellan and Burnside, and Huger was directed to halt his command at Petersburg. As his troops retired toward that city, they tore up tracks of the

Norfolk & Petersburg line and the Seaboard & Roanoke railroads east of Suffolk as far as possible and destroyed the railroad bridges to hinder pursuit. Then they marched west over the flat, peanut-growing country.

When Huger reached his new position, he found that some of the newspapers were unreasonably critical of him. They read as if he, not Johnston, had decided on the abandonment of Norfolk. Prior to the evacuation, both military and naval authorities at Norfolk had considered the defenses of the city and the south side of the James strong enough to resist an attack by water. The only apprehension felt had been that regarding the possibility of the enemy's approach by land from the area of Suffolk. Huger had written to General Lee on 3 May, "My idea is that abandoning this place is abandoning Virginia, and it would be better to sacrifice every man of us in its defense than to give it up."[14]

Huger knew the cause of the calumny from the press. Many generals welcomed newsmen on their staffs. Huger was not one of them. He explained to an inquiring friend after the war, "As I would have no editors or reporters on my staff to write me up, they combined to write me down."[15] Wise had planted a seed, and disgruntled newsmen were still taking advantage of it.

Richmond by this time was in a state bordering on panic. When war vessels had been sent up the James to bombard the capital, the move had caught the Confederates unprepared. They had counted on the *Virginia* to hold off Goldsborough's whole fleet. Drewry's Bluff, the first high ground below the city, offered a possible solution. For two months, ever since the *Monitor* had made its timely appearance in Hampton Roads, preparations at the bluff to build a fort that would stop the Union ironclad had been in progress, though the stronghold was yet incomplete. Fort Darling, the name given to the stronghold, was located on the bluff, some two hundred feet above the surface of the river, the muzzles of its heavy guns pointing downstream. Directly in front of the fort and across the water stretched a line of piles and scuttled hulks. For more than a week, a company of engineers had been occupied in placing water mines in the river as a further obstruction. Brigadier General William Mahone's brigade of Huger's command proceeded immediately by railroad to the bluff to cover the battery at Fort Darling. The brigade commander, of considerable military training and experience and formerly president, chief engineer, and superintendent of the Norfolk & Petersburg Railroad, assumed command of the post and superintended the engineering operations.

With headquarters occupying the customhouse in Petersburg, Huger's command was redesignated the Department of the Appomattox, which consisted of the Petersburg area, under Brigadier General Lewis A. Armistead, Drewry's Bluff, commanded by Mahone, and the Appomattox region, under Brigadier General Albert G. Blanchard. Huger's force for a time had been in the neighborhood of twenty thousand men incorporated in two divisions under Major Generals John C. Pemberton and W. W. Lorring. Owing to the removal of detachments sent across the James to the peninsula and those sent to strengthen the Confederates in observation of McDowell's command, the department had been reduced to the present divisional force of three brigades, about seven thousand men, the number Huger had originally found on his arrival in Norfolk a year before.

On 15 May, an armada of Union ironclads raised anchor and began moving up the James. Stationed along both banks, in rifle pits, and in treetops, Huger's sharpshooters blazed away, peppering portholes and pilothouses. The guns of Fort Darling, served by the crew of the *Virginia*, poured a crushing fire on the two ironclads in the advance. The vessels were not as formidable as had been thought. After four hours of firing, the flotilla retreated down the river. Richmond was never again seriously threatened by water.

Slowed by heavy rains, muddy roads, and a rearguard action at Williamsburg, McClellan meanwhile proceeded up the peninsula according to plan and established his base of supply at White House, expecting that McDowell would join him on the north bank of the Chickahominy River. On the twentieth, his advance crossed the river at Bottom's Bridge, less than six miles from Richmond. When Johnston learned of the crossing, he ordered Huger's command to join his army, then on the outskirts of the capital. The troops proceeded by train on the night of the twenty-eighth.

4. *Seven Pines: A Military Nightmare*

The bulk of Huger's division reached Richmond on 29 May and marched through the city on Franklin Street, passing by Capitol Square and near the offices of the War Department. Large crowds of spectators lined both sides of the street. Regimental bands played patriotic tunes as colors waved above them. The soldiers marched as if in review. They had been drilling for a year, and their exceptional discipline and precision of movement as they passed in solid columns exhibited the highest degree of proficiency and skill. The newspapers complimented them commensurately. Unfortunately, some reporters compared them to other troops who had passed through the city. This, of course, offended the others, who, being the most numerous, said and wrote all sorts of things about the division. Huger, being the commander, received the lion's share of abuse.[1]

The division halted on the outskirts of the city and went into bivouac north of Gillies Creek in the vicinity of Blakey's Mill and Oakwood Cemetery. Huger selected J. B. Williams's farmhouse for his headquarters.

A violent rainstorm set in about 5 o'clock in the afternoon the next day. Late in the evening, a messenger arrived at

47

division headquarters bearing a note from the commanding general:

> *Headquarters Department of Northern Virginia,*
> *May 30, 1862—8.40 p.m.*
>
> *Major-General Huger:*
> *General: The reports of Maj. Gen. D. H. Hill give me the impression that the enemy is in considerable strength in his front. It seems to me necessary that we should increase our force also. For that object I wish to concentrate the troops of your division on the Charles City road and concentrate the troops of Major-General Hill on that to Williamsburg. To do this it will be necessary for you to move as early in the morning as possible to relieve the brigade of General Hill's division now on the Charles City road. I have desired General Hill to send you a guide. The road is the second large one diverging to the right from the Williamsburg road; the first turns off near the toll-gate. On reaching your position on the Charles City road[,] learn at once the routes to the main roads to Richmond on your right and left, especially those to the left, and try to find guides. Be ready, if an action should be begun on your left, to fall upon the enemy's left flank.*
>
> > *Most respectfully, your obedient servant,*
> > *J. E. Johnston,*
> > *General*
>
> *P.S.— It is important to move very early.*[2]

Huger immediately sent the note to his generals, who were encamped with their brigades on the other side of Gillies Creek. Although the creek had a wide bed, normally only a narrow stream flowed between its scarped banks. Owing to the heavy rain, however, the messenger Huger had sent to bear the note had ridden over the creek going but had to swim his horse to get back, the bridge having been carried away in the torrent.

A second note was received at a very early hour the following morning:

> *Headquarters Department of Northern Virginia,*
> *May 31, 1862.*

Major-General Huger:

  General: I fear that in my note of last evening, of which there is no copy, I was too positive on the subject of your attacking the enemy's left flank. It will, of course, be necessary for you to know what force is before you first. I hope to be able to have that ascertained for you by cavalry. As our main force will be on your left, it will be necessary for your progress to the front to conform at first to that of General Hill. If you find no strong body in your front, it will be well to aid General Hill; but then a strong reserve should be retained to cover our right.

> *Yours, truly,*
> *J. E. Johnston,*
> *General*[3]

According to Johnston's instructions, the enemy was in considerable force in front of Hill's division on the Confederate right. To strengthen this weak position, Hill was to concentrate his troops on the Williamsburg Road while Huger's division was to be stationed on Hill's right to guard the extreme right of the army. If Huger found no strong body in his front, he could reinforce Hill provided that he retained a strong reserve to cover his own position. To effect the concentration of troops on the right, Brigadier General Robert E. Rodes's brigade, then in observation about three and a half miles out on the Charles City Road, was to be relieved by one of Huger's brigades so that it could rejoin Hill. It was important therefore for Huger to relieve Rodes's brigade at a very early hour.

Huger wasted no time. He sent a message an hour before daylight informing Hill that Armistead's brigade would be sent to relieve that of Rodes as soon as possible if Hill would send a guide for it, that he would notify Hill when the brigade was in motion, and that delay might occur owing to the muddy roads. Huger then rode to the camp of his division. There he had his troops break camp and load their wagons in preparation for moving to their new position. While he supervised their progress, his brigade commanders led the troops and trains.

With the last of his forces on their way, he departed camp himself to take his place at the head of the division. Spurring to the front, he was surprised to see his column halted, blocked at the crossing of Gillies Creek by thousands of other Confederate troops. The obstructing force was another division of Johnston's army under Major General James Longstreet. The head of Longstreet's division had come down the hillside on the road and had reached the crossing first. An improvised bridge had been made, but this makeshift construction— a wagon in the creek bed as a trestle with planks extended to the opposite bank—was so narrow that Longstreet's fourteen thousand men were crossing in single file.

After this force crossed, one of Longstreet's aides arrived at the scene and told Huger that his commander requested to see him at Hill's headquarters, Harrison's farmhouse.[4] There Huger was greeted by Longstreet and Hill. Longstreet told Huger that his division was moving to attack the enemy and that he desired Huger to move his troops on the Charles City Road. Huger was amazed. His two brief notes from Johnston were actually vague—extemely vague—battle orders! He replied that he had received instructions from Johnston to conduct his division on the Charles City Road but had not been informed that Longstreet's division was to join Hill's for an attack. He added that Longstreet's division occupied the crossing of the creek and had thus compelled his own command to wait until the force had passed, that his troops would follow as promptly as possible and would proceed to the position indicated by Johnston's instructions. Longstreet seemed to think that Huger's division had had previous notice to march and was therefore in advance of his division. He sent orders for his division to halt on the roadside until Huger's forces came up parallel to his.

When Longstreet claimed by instructions from Johnston to be in command of the right wing—his own, Hill's, and Huger's divisions—Huger asked: "General, which of us is the senior officer? I presume I am, but I really do not know." Longstreet replied that he was the senior. Huger protested. Could Longstreet produce the order placing him in command of the wing? No; all his orders from the commanding general had been given verbally. Longstreet remarked further that he

did not know why it should be so—from their former positions
in the "old army" it ought not to have been so—but he was the
senior. Huger had not seen mention of this in either of his two
notes from Johnston, but then the army commander had not
even informed him that a battle had been planned. He told
Longstreet that, if that officer were sure that he was his senior,
that was enough for him; he would do all in his power to assist
the wing commander. It was then possibly 10 or 11 A.M. The
conversation ended, and Huger rode back to Gillies Creek.[5]

On his return, Huger was occupied in moving his division
on as rapidly as possible. The troops marched south, passed
C. C. Williams's house, and turned left onto the Williamsburg
Road, the vanguard halting at Tudor's house.

For some reason, Mahone's men instead of Armistead's
left the intersection of the Williamsburg and Charles City
Roads to relieve Rodes's brigade. Longstreet ordered three
brigades of his division under Brigadier General Cadmus M.
Wilcox to march with Huger's column. Wilcox was directed to
follow as a support to Blanchard's and Armistead's brigades,
Huger's remaining two. After receiving instructions from the
wing commander, Huger left the Williamsburg Road with the
five brigades.

The order for Wilcox to follow Huger's column was soon
modified, and Wilcox's three brigades were ordered by
Longstreet to precede Huger's two. After Huger's brigades
were passed, the march was continued for a short time when
orders were again received from Longstreet, this time to
countermarch to the Williamsburg Road to follow in rear of the
troops then advancing. The brigades retraced their steps
almost a mile when orders were again received from Longstreet
to march back down the Charles City Road, keeping abreast of
the distant firing.

During this time, Huger remained with Armistead's and
Blanchard's brigades. Proceeding cautiously but steadily, he
moved his column on the road and reached a position previously designated by Longstreet, where a road ran across to the
Williamsburg Road. The din of heavy firing indicated that the
battle was raging northeast of his position. He placed his
troops in column and occupied the Charles City Road at that
point for several hours. His officers believed that their position

was a vital one in that it was guarding the army's right flank. But he found no enemy in his front; and as precious minutes passed in idleness, he became impatient, his every movement and the movements of his staff indicating that he was looking and waiting for orders, for mounted couriers were galloping up and dashing off.[6]

Late in the afternoon, troops on the Charles City Road were sent into the fighting by Longstreet's orders. Wilcox marched his column on county roads and paths through woods and fields to the Williamsburg Road. The march over the flooded countryside was of necessity very slow, and it was about 5 o'clock when the head of his column reached the destination. Two of Wilcox's regiments were sent into action. Meanwhile, a mounted courier came dashing up and handed a paper to Huger. As soon as his eyes fell on it, he immediately led Armistead's troops on the crossroad. When he reached the Williamsburg Road, one of his regiments, the Fifty-third Virginia, was ordered by Longstreet to remain as a reserve with him. Huger, with the reduced brigade, now not more than two thousand strong, arrived on the battlefield a little before dusk, while heavy firing raged on the Confederate left. A cavalry private wrote at the time: "I saw Gen. Longstreet and Gen. Huger on the field late in the evening and when the shells were flying the thickest and they were right in the midst of them . . . Huger was a handsome man with an extemely handsome face."[7]

Darkness ended the battle about 9 o'clock. Mahone and Blanchard were still in position with their brigades on the Charles City Road. Mahone's troops bivouacked in their present position, but Longstreet sent for Blanchard's brigade to encamp with Armistead's near the captured Union earthworks in an open field on the north side of the Williamsburg Road.

When Johnston had been severely wounded at twilight, he was succeeded by his second in command, Major General Gustavus W. Smith. In an effort to renew the battle at an early hour the following morning, 1 June, Smith ordered Longstreet to send to the front the troops of his (Longstreet's) and Huger's divisions who had not been engaged the day before. Longstreet directed Mahone's brigade to proceed at daylight to the Nine Mile Road to report to Hill and ordered Huger to conduct Blanchard's brigade to a position on the left of the Williamsburg Road, where the men were posted in reserve. Armistead's brigade was on the immediate right of Mahone's and both struck the enemy about the same time. Friends and enemies became so indiscriminately mixed in the dense woods that some Confederates mistakenly fired at each other, apprehending more danger from themselves than from the Federals. One of Longstreet's brigades was also engaged, but the three under Wilcox exchanged little fire with the enemy. About 3 o'clock in the afternoon, Huger, under orders from Longstreet, conducted Blanchard's brigade to the front and turned the command over to Hill. Then he returned to his headquarters.

Arriving in the early afternoon to succeed Johnston, General Lee ordered the troops to cease fire and remove captured property. By evening, the Confederates were abandoning the Union works. Huger's division alone was left in the front, extending from the Richmond & York River Railroad across the Williamsburg Road to beyond the Charles City Road, to check all attempts of the enemy to advance.

As early as when the Confederates were withdrawing to their former position, a rumor had spread rapidly through the army and was being circulated in Richmond by wounded soldiers who reported it to the citizens. It was alleged that the failure of Huger to lead his division into action at the appointed time was the only reason why McClellan's left wing had not been completely destroyed. The rumor passed to the press, and newspapers were soon asserting it.

In order to gain an understanding of the circumstances under which the rumor originated, it will be necessary to retrace the events of the battle in greater detail. By 24 May, the five corps of McClellan's army were occupying a front partly encircling Richmond on the north and east. Three corps were north of the Chickahominy River in anticipation of McDowell's approach from Fredericksburg, while the two corps under Brigadier Generals Erasmus D. Keys and Samuel P. Heintzelman were south of the river. Because of Major General Stonewall Jackson's brilliant operations in the Shenandoah Valley threatening Washington, McDowell's orders to join

McClellan were temporarily suspended, though McClellan still kept his right wing across the river, which dangerously split the two wings.

Learning of the enemy's predicament, Johnston determined to destroy Keyes's corps in its more advanced position on the Williamsburg Road before it could be reinforced by that of Heintzelman or by forces sent south across the Chickahominy. D. H. Hill's division was to proceed east on the Williamsburg Road, and Longstreet was to move his division on the Nine Mile Road, the forces to converge at the junction of the two roads, known as Seven Pines. While Hill's division would attack along the Williamsburg Road, that of Longstreet was to engage Keyes's forces on Hill's left. Smith's division was to move on the Nine Mile Road to be in easy supporting distance of the other two divisions. As previously noted, Huger's division was to advance southeast on the Charles City Road to protect the Confederate right flank. Probably because this division had the longest march, the time for the opening of the battle was to be set by Huger. As soon as his relief brigade reached Rodes's position, the brigade there was to join its division, at which time signal guns were to be fired. Immediately, Hill's division was to attack. Longstreet, on hearing Hill's fire, was to engage the enemy in his front. Johnston intended for his divisions to move at daylight (about 4 o'clock) on 31 May to their assigned positions, expecting that Keyes's corps would be crushed or routed by 8 A.M. Unfortunately, he never consulted Huger, never informed him of any plan of battle, never intimated that he intended to attack at all. But this was not the principal factor which enabled Keyes's corps to escape annihilation.

Longstreet believed Johnston to be the greatest soldier of the South, and the two were intimate friends. Moreover, Longstreet thought of himself as the senior officer from Alabama who had left the United States service, although Major General David E. Twiggs was actually the senior. In any event, he determined that his seniority should be respected and that no junior should be promoted over him except for gallantry. Hence, when Smith's position had changed from street commissioner of New York City to ranking major general, he had been outraged.[8] He had doubtless felt that he, not the "big name"[9] newcomer, should be second in command to his friend. When Huger appeared in Johnston's army, Longstreet's seniority problem doubled. He decided to get rid of his two seniors by having them blamed for failing to destroy Keyes's corps.[10]

Johnston worked out his detailed plan of battle in a long conference with Longstreet on the thirtieth, and it was at that time that the conniving junior made his first move. Smith had been given command of the left wing of the army two days earlier, the immediate command of his own division devolving on the senior brigadier, W. H. C. Whiting. Longstreet now persuaded Johnston to extend his command to include Hill's division. Hill had been one of his brigade commanders earlier in the war, and he had been in command of his own and Hill's divisions during their march from Williamsburg when the army had been withdrawing up the peninsula. Johnston stipulated, however, that control would revert from Longstreet when the two divisions converged at Seven Pines, where he would be present to direct the movements, after which each major general would command his own division.[11]

Instead of advancing on the Nine Mile Road according to Johnston's plan, Longstreet transferred his division to the Williamsburg Road. This would enable him to escape Smith's seniority, delay the attack, gain control of Huger, and occupy a position where he could accomplish his object. With the view of establishing himself on the right permanently, he moved all his troops and all their baggage and camp equipment, together with the artillery, ordnance, and ambulance trains. Since the division spread some distance on the Nine Mile Road from its main camp on Fairfield Racecourse, he countermarched the troops below the racecourse up the Nine Mile Road and turned the head of his division southward. By his doing this and taking all his wagons along, Whiting's division, moving to its assigned position on the Nine Mile Road, was delayed for two or three hours.

Whiting, having been ordered to move his men as early as possible to a point more than four miles distant, wrote to Johnston requesting that the route be cleared. He was answered that Longstreet was to precede him on the Nine Mile Road. This quieted him for a time; but as the delay continued, he became impatient and rode to army headquarters, where Smith had previously ridden. There he asked Smith to put an end to the delay. Smith directed First Lieutenant Robert F. Becham, one of his aides, to see Longstreet in regard to the matter. Johnston, when asked by Becham where Longstreet was, said that Longstreet's division was out on the Nine Mile Road and that its commander was probably with it. In about an hour, Becham reported that neither Longstreet nor any of his troops were on the Nine Mile Road. Johnston, skeptical of this report that Longstreet was not on his assigned road, directed Whiting to order his division to remain where it was until the position of Longstreet's division was established. He then sent one of his aides, First Lieutenant James B. Washington (a great-great-grandnephew of George Washington), on the Nine Mile Road to find Longstreet. Failing to find Longstreet there, he was to go to the Williamsburg Road and tell that officer to send three brigades back to the Nine Mile Road, unless they had moved so far that there would be a serious loss of time in returning them. But Washington unwittingly rode into the enemy's picket line and was captured.

It was during this time that the head of Longstreet's column, moving southward, reached Gillies Creek. Previously, Longstreet had directed Hill to move his division on the Williamsburg Road and to lead the attack against the enemy. But he had specifically ordered Hill not to begin the attack until the relief brigade from Huger reached Rodes's position. At this time, his division was blocking Huger's. If Longstreet, General R. E. Colston later wrote, "had given orders for the men to sling their cartridge-boxes, haversacks, etc., on their muskets and wade without breaking formation, they could have crossed [the creek] by fours at least, with water up to their waists . . . and hours would have been saved . . . When we got across[,] we received orders to halt on the roadside until Huger's division passed us. There we waited for five or six hours."[12] Huger wrote: "I regretted the delay as much as any one [else] and did all in my power to expedite the movement."[13] "If I had been notified [that] Longstreet['s division] was to pass, I would have made another crossing; even then, if Genl Johnston had told me his plan, I would have left the trains [of my division] to follow, & swam the men over. [But] I only knew [that] I was to change position, and it was not until after Genl L's crossing [that] I was informed by him, my junior, that he had Johnston's instructions to attack the enemy."[14]

At Hill's headquarters, Longstreet asserted that Johnston had placed him in command of the right wing, grossly exaggerating the actual agreement. Knowing that Huger was his senior, he offered that officer an ingenious lie—that Huger had been senior to him in the "old army" but that he was senior to Huger in the Confederate army. The first part of the statement was true: having been promoted to major before Longstreet, Huger had been his senior in the United States service. Both officers had been elevated to brigadier and major general in the Confederate army on the same days. Hence, if their dates of commission were compared, the comparison would have tended to confirm Longstreet's assertion. Only records at the adjutant general's office could determine seniority. At the moment, there was a battle to be fought.[15]

Not long after the wing commander and his two division commanders left Harrison's farmhouse, Lieutenant Becham found Longstreet at his new headquarters (Poe's house) and saw that Longstreet's division was halted on the Williamsburg Road for the purpose of allowing Huger's troops (which he mistakenly reported as Hill's) to file by. Becham reported this by courier to Smith, who repeated it to Johnston. Johnston muttered that he wished all the troops were back in camp. Then he told Smith that the "misunderstanding" over Longstreet's route of advance might be his fault, not Longstreet's. But Johnston's sense of honor and his affection for Longstreet led him to shoulder the responsibility.[16] Without further discussion, he ordered Whiting's division to take the place that had been assigned to Longstreet's.

If Huger had notified Hill when the relief brigade had left camp, as he had promised to do in his 3 A.M. message, that brigade was about eight hours late. At 1 o'clock, some two hours later, Longstreet sent orders to Hill to begin the attack regardless of the "delay" of Huger's troops. At the sound of the signal guns, the relief brigade moved to Rodes's vacated position. Longstreet ordered three of his brigades forward from the rear of his column, thereby further delaying Huger's troops, who stood on the side of the road to allow the brigades to pass. Huger's column then left the Williamsburg Road. After reaching a point on the Charles City Road which seemed to have been designated, the column took position in line of battle, though there was no enemy in the vicinity, and waited for signal guns to be fired on the left by those of Longstreet's men who were marching to the front on the Williamsburg Road. It was probably about 3:30 P.M. when the signal was heard. Drastically modifying Johnston's orders to Huger, Longstreet directed that officer, on reaching a position down the road designated by him, to *wait for further orders.*[17]

After Hill's division had been actively engaged for nearly three hours, President Davis and members of his cabinet joined Longstreet and Hill on the field. Longstreet told the group that, according to Johnston's plan of battle, Huger was to have *attacked the enemy's left flank and rear* and pretended to be mortified at Huger's inactivity. Davis and the cabinet members were naturally perplexed at Huger's "slowness" and rode from point to point anxiously expecting to hear his guns open fire.[18]

Longstreet gave McClellan ample time to reinforce Keyes's corps. Heintzelman's corps hurried forward over muddy roads, and Brigadier General Edwin V. Sumner's corps crossed the Chickahominy from the north on Grapevine Bridge and continued rapidly to the battlefield.

Longstreet wrote a message to Johnston at this time, about 4 o'clock. The message read that he had attacked and beaten the enemy after several hours of severe fighting, that he had been disappointed in not receiving assistance from his left (Whiting's division, controlled by Smith), and although it was now nearly too late, that an attack by the Nine Mile Road (from Smith) on the enemy's right and rear flanks would prob-ably enable him to drive the enemy into the Chickahominy before night. Peculiar atmospheric conditions and the dense woods so muffled the noise of battle that Hill's fire was not heard on the left until after 4 o'clock. While Johnston's plan was to engage the enemy by a simultaneous attack with his right and left, Longstreet tried to make it appear as if his wing constituted Johnston's whole plan and that Whiting's division was merely to support his left. At this time, he was keeping eight of his thirteen brigades out of battle and had not made and was not making any drive against the enemy. But with this message, Smith and Huger could be blamed for the failure of his fictitious drive. The message could be used as evidence against Smith for failing to annihilate the enemy's right flank and rear during the "several hours of severe fighting." With Davis, cabinet members, Hill, and others as witnesses, Huger could be blamed for failing to bring his division to the front at the "proper time" to crush the enemy's left flank and rear. After the battle, one of Longstreet's aides saw his commander, Davis, Navy Secretary Mallory, Whiting, and others and later commented to a friend that they had appeared to be "as mad as thunder" at Huger's "slowness."[19]

Longstreet had attacked with four brigades (Hill's) and ended with four brigades (three of Hill's and one of his own). Except for one break, the Federals had not been driven back as a force at any time during the day. On Hill's left, troops of Sumner's corps had easily repulsed Whiting's attacks. The next day Longstreet made only a feeble attempt to obey Smith's order to renew the attack and was not even on the field to direct operations.

As soon as the battle was over, Huger sent an officer to Richmond to ask at the adjutant general's office for an official list of general officers according to seniority. The officer returned without the list, however. When the army had fallen back from Yorktown, the public documents had been packed in boxes and sent away. Huger wrote vaguely, "I applied to Genl Lee, and from what the Presdt afterwards told me, he had been consulted about it, but I could get no satisfaction for weeks."[20]

Late in the evening of 31 May, it will be recalled, Huger was directed by Longstreet to send Mahone's brigade early the next morning to report to Hill. By the time morning came, Armistead was already under Hill; and that afternoon, Huger, by Longstreet's orders, conducted Blanchard's brigade to the front and reported it to Hill. Thus were the three brigades of his division taken from him, one by one. The next day he addressed a letter to the new commanding general:

> *Headquarters Huger's Division*
> *June 2, 1862*
>
> *General R. E. Lee,*
>   *Commanding:*
>   *General: I beg to call your attention to the fact that all the troops I commanded have been detached, I presume from the necessity of the service; and finding myself on the field last evening without any command at all, I, with the permission of General Longstreet, returned to these headquarters.*
>   *The First Brigade of my division (Colston's) was detached to reinforce General Magruder when the enemy first advanced up the Peninsula. The three brigades I brought up with me are at present serving under the orders of Major-General Hill.*
>   *I ask that all may be returned to my command. I hope the position I am placed in is merely an accidental one, and will be changed as soon as it can be done.*
>   *I must demand the position and command my rank entitles me to. On no other condition will I hold it.*
>   *I am, very respectfully, your obedient servant,*
>   *Benj. Huger,*
>   *Major-General*[21]

On 3 June, Lee forwarded the letter to Longstreet with an endorsement directing him to prepare "a report of the facts in the case."

Longstreet had apparently detached Huger's division from its commander to give color to rumor. On 2 June, he had relieved Hill from commanding the division and had placed it under Brigadier General J. E. B. Stuart, chief of the army's cavalry. Instead of explaining why he had taken the division away from Huger and had put it under Hill, he very briefly explained why he had placed Stuart in command of the division. After quickly reinstating Huger to command, he endorsed on the letter—rather than submitting a separate and full report:

> The entire division of General Huger was left in advance upon retiring with the forces from the late battlefield.

He was absent yesterday, and not coming to report after being sent for, I ordered General Stuart to take the command of the division during the absence of General Huger.

He has joined his division this morning and taken command.[22]

This made it appear that Huger had been negligent. As if to placate that officer, he furnished Huger additional brigades to assist in performing picket duty and placed all of his own troops at Huger's disposal.[23]

As far as Longstreet was concerned, his 4 o'clock message to Johnston was enough to discredit Smith; but his charges against Huger should also be in writing. In a letter to Johnston acknowledging the receipt of a gift from his wounded friend, then confined to his bed, he accordingly wrote on 7 June:

The failure of complete success on Saturday [31 May] I attribute to the slow movements of General Huger's command. This threw perhaps the hardest part of the battle upon my own poor division. It is greatly cut up, but as true and ready as ever. Our ammunition was nearly exhausted when Whiting moved, and I could not therefore move on with the rush that we could had his movement been earlier. . .

I can't but help think that a display of his forces on the left flank of the enemy by General Huger would have completed the affair and given Whiting as easy and pretty a game as was ever had upon a battle-field. Slow men are a little out of place upon the field. Altogether it was very well, but I can't help but regret that it was not complete.[24]

Longstreet soon found that Johnston, not Smith, had been in command on the Nine Mile Road; and the criticism of the lack of support not only reflected adversely on his friend, but at the same time, exposed the fact that he had not been on his assigned road. Hence, he could not blame Smith. Besides, Smith's seniority was not as threatening as before. The second in command had suffered a paralytic stroke the day after the battle. Instead, Longstreet persuaded Johnston to side with him to prevent him from being blamed for the Confederate failure which he had deliberately caused; and the two entered into a collusion to place the entire blame on Huger.

In his official report of the battle, dated 10 June, Longstreet confirmed the rumor which he had originated:

> The division of Major-General Huger was intended to make a strong flank movement around the left of the enemy's position and attack him in rear of that flank. This division did not get into position, however, in time for any such attack, and I was obliged to send three of my small brigades on the Charles City road to support the one of Major-General Huger's which had been ordered to protect my right flank.
>
> After waiting some six hours for these troops to get into position[,] I determined to move forward without regard to them, and gave orders to that effect to Maj. Gen. D. H. Hill. . . .
>
> Some of the brigades of Major-General Huger's division took part in defending our position on Sunday, but, being fresh at work, did not show the same steadiness and determination as the troops of Hill's division and my own.
>
> I have reason to believe that the affair would have been a complete success had the troops upon the right been put into position within eight hours of the proper time. The want of promptness on that part of the field and the consequent severe struggle in my front so greatly reduced my supply of ammunition, that at the late hour of the move on the left [by Whiting] I was unable to make the rush necessary to relieve that attack.[25]

Longstreet added, "Detailed reports of the major-generals, brigadiers, and other commanders and chiefs of staff have been called for and will be forwarded as soon as received."[26] But he made no effort to call for official reports which would conflict with his own version of the battle, as neither Huger nor any of his officers filed a report.

Johnston, entirely ignorant of Huger's movements

merely rephrased Longstreet's false statements in his official report, dated 24 June:

> General Huger, with his division, was to move down the Charles City road in order to attack in flank the troops who might be engaged with Hill and Longstreet, unless he found in his front force enough to occupy his division. . . .
>
> Major-General Longstreet, unwilling to make a partial attack, instead of the combined movement which had been planned, waited from hour to hour for General Huger's division. At length, at 2 p.m., he determined to attack without those troops. . . .
>
> Had Major-General Huger's division been in position and ready for action when those of Smith, Longstreet, and Hill moved, I am satisfied that Keyes' corps would have been destroyed instead of being merely defeated. Had it gone into action even at 4 o'clock[,] the victory would have been much more complete.[27]

As might be expected, both reports asserted that Longstreet was supposed to conduct his division to Hill's position on the Williamsburg Road; and while severely censuring the "slowness" of Huger's division, they were silent in regard to the cause of delay. When Smith's official report was submitted to Johnston, that officer returned it with the request for Smith to omit the preliminary movements, which exposed the fact that Longstreet had been on the wrong road, and to strike out his reference to the 4 o'clock message.

In general orders dated 2 June, Longstreet had stated, "The commanding general congratulates the troops of Maj. Gen. D. H. Hill and his own upon their handsome conduct" during the two days of battle. "The [name] Seven Pines will be inscribed on the regimental banners of each regiment of the two divisions, except those few regiments that disgracefully left the battle-field with their colors. The Seven Pines will also be inscribed upon the standard of the Fifty-third Regiment Virginia Volunteers of General Armistead's brigade, Major-General Huger's division." Naturally, Huger was disturbed to see in congratulatory orders such scant recognition of the service of his own troops. When he called attention to this, Longstreet made all the excuse in his power, ordered that "Seven Pines" be inscribed on the flags of more of Huger's regiments, and published a general order on the twelfth (two days after the date of his report), in which he stated that at the publication of the preceding general order, "the extent of the service of Major-General Huger's division was not understood. That division is entitled to its share of the honors of the day."[28]

Longstreet, whose conduct at Seven Pines bordered on treason, emerged not only blameless but with prestige increased. The published official reports led the southern people to put his name above all those genuinely distinguished on that field of confusion. On the other hand, the first great battle in the East left in widespread distrust the abilities of General Huger, who was already unpopular for having refused to take command in his native state, for having allegedly caused the disaster at Roanoke Island, and for having allegedly deserted Norfolk.

5. *King's Schoolhouse: On the Defensive*

Longstreet lost no time in playing the role of second in command after Seven Pines. He moved into part of the house that Lee was using as his headquarters and quickly developed a close friendship with the new commanding general. Throughout the remainder of the campaign, he was always to be seen with Lee, accompanying him on the march and bivouacking his command near army headquarters.[1]

Before the Battle of Seven Pines, the Federal blockade along the coast had sealed off all the important southern ports with the exception of Charleston, Savannah, Wilmington, and Mobile. The capture of Charleston would close that channel of the South's communication with the foreign world, on which the Confederacy depended in great measure for valuable cargoes of food, clothing, and munitions. Conditions for the defense of the city at this time were deplorable. Commanding the coastal defenses from South Carolina to Florida with headquarters in Charleston was Lee's successor, Major General John C. Pemberton. Because of his northern birth and his impartiality to the city's people of importance and lesser standing alike, Charlestonians were suspicious of his loyalty to the South. On 23 May, Governor Pickens wrote to Lee, "we want a new man of large experience who will talk and act like a

hero and raise the enthusiasm of our people." He requested
that Huger be sent to relieve Pemberton. Lee replied on the
twenty-ninth that Huger could not be spared from Johnston's
army. "I esteem him very highly," he added, "and he has
always been regarded as an officer of great merit, especially as
an artillerist."[2]

Longstreet viewed the situation in Charleston as an opportunity to get rid of Huger. To Lee, he doubtless reinforced the
charges against Huger for the failure on 31 May and urged
that that officer be relieved by R. H. Anderson, Longstreet's
senior brigade commander. Lee informed Davis on 19 June
that Huger could be spared from his army. Five days later the
president discussed the possibility with Huger. Longstreet's
opportunity was short-lived, however. Huger evidently declined,
probably because the feeling in South Carolina against him
was still strong.[3]

Soon after taking command of what he christened the
Army of Northern Virginia, Lee ordered the construction of
earthworks to extend south from the Chickahominy River to a
point just below the Charles City Road. While the defensive
line of entrenchments and redoubts was being dug for Huger's
and Magruder's troops, the enemy corps opposing the Confederate front were similarly occupied in strengthening and
enlarging their earthworks.

Believing that he had to deal with twice his numbers,
McClellan determined to advance from position to position
until his superior siege guns forced the evacuation of Richmond.
Anticipating this, Lee hoped to turn McClellan's right flank
north of the Chickahominy and cut his supply route, the
Richmond & York River Railroad from White House. Without
food and munitions, the Federals would be forced out of their
fieldworks to give battle in the open or to retreat. On 12 June,
Lee sent Stuart's cavalry to reconnoiter McClellan's right and
to report on the feasibility of his contemplated attack. Instead
of retiring from White House the way he had gone, Stuart
exceeded his instructions by riding around McClellan's whole
army, returning to Richmond on the fifteenth by way of the
James. The expedition alerted McClellan to the danger of his
extended flank and base of supply. The Federal commander
began preparations to change his base from White House to

Harrison's Landing by the James and moved Brigadier General William B. Franklin's corps south of the Chickahominy. Only the corps of Brigadier General Fitz John Porter remained on the north side to connect with McDowell's should it finally arrive.

Receiving from Stuart convincing information that the north flank could be turned, Lee developed the plan for his counteroffensive. He would quickly and secretly bring Major General Stonewall Jackson's command from the Shenandoah Valley, and with the bulk of his army north of the Chickahominy, overwhelm Porter's corps on 26 June. In round numbers, this meant that he would concentrate sixty-five thousand troops against Porter's thirty thousand. To protect the capital, he would leave the twenty-five thousand effectives of Huger and Magruder in their earthworks to hold in check the seventy-five thousand men of the four Federal corps south of the river. On the proposed day of battle, the Confederates on the south side would demonstrate in order to deceive the enemy in their front.

On the morning of 25 June, McClellan began an advance with the object of testing the strength of the Confederates opposite his left in preparation of a more powerful advance the next day by Franklin's corps in the direction of Old Tavern. Heintzelman's corps, with elements from Sumner and Keyes, engaged Huger's division in a savage but relatively localized fight, the first in a sequence soon to be known as the Seven Days' Battles. Huger's division was reinforced by a brigade from D. H. Hill and a brigade from the Department of North Carolina, the latter, under Brigadier General Robert Ransom, being attached to the division for the remainder of the campaign. There were many instances of hand-to-hand fighting, and the trophies taken by Huger's troops included the colors of the famed Excelsior Brigade and two cannons. The Battle of King's Schoolhouse, as the Confederates called it, closed at dark with Huger reestablishing his advance line of pickets and Heintzelman preparing his men to fight behind their earthworks.

Despite McClellan's activity, Lee made no change in the plan for his counteroffensive. Jackson's command was to march from Ashland on the twenty-fifth and encamp for the night just west of the Virginia Central Railroad. At early dawn the next day, he was to advance and envelope Porter's right flank at Beaver Dam Creek. Major General A. P. Hill's division was to cross the Chickahominy at the Meadow Bridges when Jackson's advance beyond that point would become known and move directly on Mechanicsville. This would clear the area of Mechanicsville Bridge of Federals; and the divisions of Longstreet and D. H. Hill would cross the Chickahominy, the latter to proceed to the support of Jackson and the former to that of A. P. Hill. With Jackson in advance, the four commands would then move in echelon to overwhelm Porter's corps.

As 26 June wore on with no word from Jackson, however, A. P. Hill became impatient and fearful for the success of Lee's plan. Without authority, he began the attack at three that afternoon and drove the enemy's outposts from Mechanicsville to a previously prepared position behind Beaver Dam Creek. Longstreet's and D. H. Hill's troops crowded behind those of A. P. Hill, who hurled his brigades forward in a hopeless and costly frontal assault against Brigadier General George A. McCall's division, previously brought from McDowell's corps and attached to Porter's. About 5 o'clock, Jackson, delayed by obstructed roads, destroyed bridges, constant skirmishing, and the fatigue of his weary troops, reached a point less than three miles northeast of where the battle was raging. By then the surprise appearance of his command was lost. But still worse, not finding A. P. Hill on his right or D. H. Hill in support as he had planned, Jackson did not know what action to take and therefore made no attempt to turn Porter's flank. The enemy withdrew during the night and early morning to another previously prepared position behind Boatswain Swamp, near Gaines' Mill.

After repairing the bridges over Beaver Dam Creek on the morning of the twenty-seventh, the several Confederate columns resumed their march, those of Jackson and D. H. Hill on the left, A. P. Hill's in the center, and Longstreet's on the right. Lee formulated another strategy. While A. P. Hill's division would attack the center of the Union line, Longstreet would make a feint on the enemy's left. Lee believed that, when Jackson's men appeared on the Federal right, Porter would shift a portion of his troops to meet the threat in order to prevent Jackson from getting between the Federal corps and its base at White House. As soon as Porter did this, Longstreet would turn his demonstration into an attack, and together with Hill, drive the enemy into Jackson and D. H. Hill, whose troops would be waiting on the Confederate left.

A. P. Hill attacked about half past two in the afternoon. Under a devastating fire, however, his division was repulsed with heavy losses. Longstreet, realizing that his feint was not helping Hill, launched a full assault but was likewise repelled with terrible slaughter. Due to a misunderstanding between himself and his guide, Jackson was again delayed, countermarching about four miles. Felled trees across his route and detachments of sharpshooters defending the obstructions added to the delay and caused him to make a detour, which placed the command in rear of D. H. Hill's division. On reaching this position, Jackson waited with his command to intercept the forces that Longstreet and A. P. Hill might drive in that direction, not knowing that the attack of those commanders had been checked. About an hour before dark, the Confederates began a combined attack along their whole front. The enemy was driven back after severe fighting. Owing to the disorganization of the southern troops after the breakthrough, approaching darkness, and ignorance of the country, no attempt was made to pursue the enemy farther.

During these operations north of the Chickahominy, Magruder frequently consulted Huger, his senior on the right; and together they examined their entire line with great care and devised many methods of exhibiting an aggressive strength in an effort to deceive McClellan. Officers shouted commands to imaginary units, buglers sounded meaningless calls, wagons rumbled back and forth over the same screened area to give the impression of an endless train, soldiers were marched in circles by clearings in sight of the enemy and returned to the scene again and again, campfires were built for nonexistent soldiers, and sound effects were utilized. And by energetically maneuvering and firing, they convinced McClellan that a Federal attack south of the Chickahominy could not be successful.

With his army now cut off from its established line of supplies, McClellan was pressed to either move at once or starve.

70

Huger about the time of his first European tour.
He was then a second lieutenant, contrary to the rank
depicted in this miniature by Charles Fraser.
Collection of the late Julie (Huger) Monniche, Austin, Texas.

The storming of Chapultepec. From a color lithograph published by
Sarony and Major of New York City in 1848. Library of Congress.

Fort Sumter before the outbreak of hostilities. From a painting by
Seth Eastman. Collection of the Architect of the Capitol.

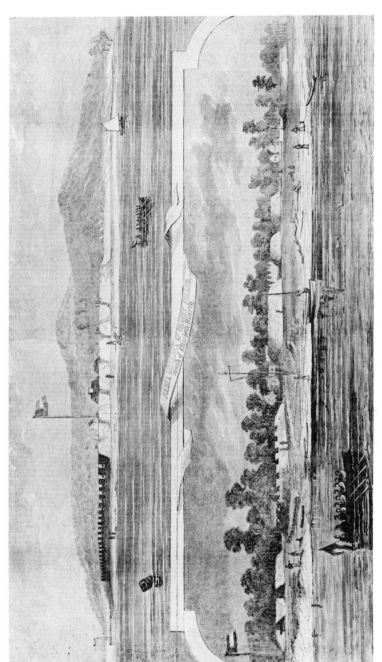

Huger's batteries on Craney Island and Sewell's Point.
From sketches made at the time. *Harper's Weekly* 2 November 1861.

Mrs. Benjamin Huger during the Civil War. Despite her lovely appearance (Robert E. Lee called her "beautiful little madam"), Celly always objected to her likeness being made. Perhaps she sat for this daguerreotype because the bonnet, which she designed and made, won the praise of her friends. Collection of the late Aurelia (Huger) Rutherfoord, Charlottesville, Virginia.

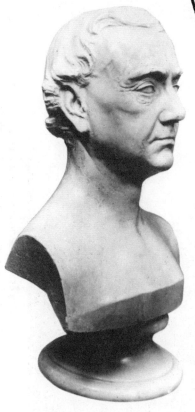

Huger at the height of his fame. This plaster bust by an unknown sculptor is considered to be the finest example of Huger's actual appearance. Collection of the late Aurelia (Huger) Rutherfoord, Charlottesville, Virginia.

Burnside's expedition passing between the marshes near Roanoke
Island. From a sketch in *Frank Leslie's Illustrated Newspaper*
8 March 1862 by an artist who accompanied the expedition.
Kean Archives, Philadelphia, Pennsylvania.

A view of the duel between the ironclads *Monitor* and *Virginia*.
The *Monitor* appears on the left, the *Virginia (Merrimac)* on the right.
Kean Archives, Philadelphia, Pennsylvania.

A view of White Oak Swamp. From a Mathew Brady photograph
taken in June 1862. Library of Congress.

Slocum's artillery opposing Huger's passage of White Oak Swamp. From a sketch made at the time by Alfred R. Waud. Kean Archives, Philadelphia, Pennsylvania.

Panorama of the Battle of Malvern Hill. From a watercolor by

Huger as president
of an iron company.
From a photograph
by Sarony and Co. of
New York City.
Collection of the late
Aurelia (Huger)
Rutherfoord,
Charlottesville,
Virginia.

Huger two years before his death. This photograph was taken in
1875 while Huger was in New York City attending what would be
his last reunion of veteran officers of Scott's Campaign of the
Mexican War (the Aztec Club), of which he was a past president.
Courtesy of the late Lucelia H. Peyton, Richmond, Virginia.

6. *White Oak Swamp: The Pursuit Blunders*

During the night of 28 June, the Federals south of the Chickahominy were quiet; and Huger suspected that they were retiring. President Davis, visiting the commands along the entrenchments, spoke with Huger and Magruder. He expressed his opinion that the enemy would begin to retreat before morning and gave special instructions regarding taking the precautions needed to hear when the movement began.

Learning during the night that his pickets were hearing wagons moving off, Huger ordered his picket regiments to advance and to push scouts forward to the Union works at daylight, the twenty-ninth, to give information of the enemy's actions. With no report coming from them after sunrise, he rode forward through the thick fog to his advance pickets. There he met Colonel George Doles of the Fourth Georgia, who had just come to the conclusion that the enemy had left. A white flag was seen flying above the works. Huger rode forward with one aide-de-camp and a company of Doles's regiment, entering the works as soon as Heintzelman's corps abandoned them.[1] He saw large quantities of military stores of every description either abandoned or destroyed—tents left standing but slashed, heaps of broken medicine bottles with their contents drenching the ground, beef smoldering in ashes. A few soldiers who represented themselves as hospital attendants were the only persons left behind. Huger was told that a surgeon was left with the sick. He rode on, found the surgeon, read his order, and told him that he would not be considered a prisoner of war.

By this time, the pickets had advanced to the works; and Huger rode along the lines, announcing that the enemy had abandoned the position and that the division was to pursue the fleeing forces on the Charles City Road. Mahone's brigade led the march, followed by the brigades of Armistead, Ransom, and then Ambrose R. Wright (formerly Blanchard's).

Lee came to the south side of the Chickahominy to unite his army and direct its movements. While the Union army retreated along the Williamsburg Road, he formulated a plan for the pursuit of the enemy. Magruder's command was to attack McClellan's rear guard for the purpose of arresting the retreat, while Jackson (commanding his own, Whiting's, D. H. Hill's, and Richard S. Ewell's divisions) was to recross the Chickahominy at Grapevine Bridge to join the attack on Magruder's left. To intercept the retreat, four Confederate columns were to converge for battle the next day, 30 June. While Jackson's powerful command (Magruder's troops being held in reserve) would strike McClellan's rear, Huger's division, marching on the Charles City Road, would hit the right flank. Longstreet (commanding his own and A. P. Hill's divisions), after recrossing the Chickahominy at New Bridge and moving on the Darbytown Road toward the Long Bridge Road, would attack McClellan's marching column in front. Major General Theophilus H. Holmes's division (originally the Department of North Carolina), crossing the James from Drewry's Bluff on the twenty-ninth and moving on the New Market Road, would get between the Federals and the James. It was thought that, by this plan, the enemy would be destroyed or captured.

After repeating the plan of battle to Magruder at Fair Oaks Station, Lee rode to division headquarters at J. B. Williams's farmhouse to inform Huger of the details. This done and on the departure of Huger and his staff, he established his headquarters in the house, from which he would direct operations that day.

When Magruder reached the vicinity of Savage Station

about noon, he came on McClellan's rear guard, halted his command, and deployed his men in execution of Lee's plan. Mistaking the resistance his command met for a renewal of the enemy's movement against Richmond, he sent a staff officer toward Grapevine Bridge to learn the position of Jackson's command, which he supposed had already recrossed the Chickahominy to cooperate on his left, and sent another staff officer, Major Joseph L. Brent, to Lee with a request that Huger's division, which he erroneously believed was marching along the Williamsburg Road on his right flank, be ordered to reinforce him, informing the commanding general and Huger that the enemy was advancing toward him in great force.

Major Brent delivered the message to Lee at Huger's late headquarters. Lee seemed surprised and skeptical at Magruder's report that the enemy was in force in his front and advancing on his command. Lee said his information was that the enemy was in rapid retreat, and he thought that the rear guard would scarcely deliver battle at Magruder's present position beyond Fair Oaks Station. Then he asked Brent if the enemy were really in large force in Magruder's front, but the loyal staff officer declined to express an opinion. After some consideration and reflection, Lee said: "Tell General Magruder that General Huger is much needed to carry out an important duty, from which he cannot be spared, but I will order him to detach two of his brigades to report to General Magruder. But if they are not actually engaged by 2 o'clock, he must order them to resume their march and rejoin General Huger on the Charles City Road."[2]

In the meantime, the staff officer sent by Magruder to Jackson returned with the latter's engineer, who reported that his commander had to rebuild Grapevine Bridge, which had been destroyed by the enemy. The bridge, he said, would be completed in about two hours, or about 2 o'clock. This delay was not anticipated. Magruder would be temporarily deprived of Jackson's expected cooperation, and the delay naturally caused him much anxiety. About the same time, he received a message from Huger that that officer would march to the Williamsburg Road with two brigades. Determined to await Huger's arrival, he planned to capture the rear guard by an attack in front and on both flanks, employing Huger's men to protect his right flank.

Huger personally conducted Ransom's brigade to Seven Pines. Taking a bypath, the head of Wright's brigade soon marched into the vacated Union works, where the commander received orders from Huger to wait for further instructions.

Magruder galloped up to Huger, on the latter's arrival, insisted that the enemy was advancing in great force, and requested his senior to form the troops in line of battle with their left on the Richmond & York River Railroad and their right at Seven Pines.

Huger had begun moving Ransom's three thousand men through the woods into position when he saw a line of other Confederate troops in his front. Inquiring what command it was, he was told that it was one of Magruder's. At the same moment, he received a dispatch from Lee stating that it was very important that he should return the two brigades to the Charles City Road, and that if his assistance were not necessary to Magruder, he was to start the brigades on their way immediately. As the Federals had abandoned their works and retired, he could not conceive that their attack was a serious one but that the demonstration was only to delay the pursuit. Furthermore, as a portion of Magruder's troops occupied the ground, Huger felt that he might leave and accordingly sent to Magruder that, under his orders, he had decided that it was not necessary for the two brigades to remain. Then about 2 o'clock, he sent orders to Wright to return his brigade to the Charles City Road and sent Ransom's in the same direction at once. "The day was intensely hot," he wrote, "and this marching and counter-marching exhausted the men."[3]

After Magruder received Huger's message, a note reached him from one of his generals stating that Jackson regretted that he could not cooperate with Magruder's left, as he had "other important duty" to perform. Jackson's "other important duty" was probably the rebuilding of Grapevine Bridge, but Magruder interpreted the "other duty" from an earlier order from Lee to Jackson as one directing Jackson's command to move elsewhere. The order referred to was probably that directing Ewell's division of Jackson's command to move to Bottom's Bridge, not an order directing Jackson's whole command to move there.[4] (In this regard, it will be recalled that Magruder had also misunderstood the order governing Huger's movement.) Magruder therefore determined to advance slowly, counting on Jackson's arrival not later than 4 o'clock. His troops were occasionally meeting Federal outposts and scouting parties, which they pressed back. The slowness of his advance indicated his desire not to force the fighting until Jackson had the opportunity to cross the Chickahominy and unite with him for the combined attack which had been planned.

It was probably about 4 o'clock when the Federals began to strengthen their pickets and make firmer opposition to his advance, but his men continually pressed them back. Then the skirmishers on both sides were withdrawn, leaving the lines of battle face to face.

With Grapevine Bridge repaired,[5] Jackson, accompanied by his staff and an infantry force, crossed the Chickahominy, and passing on the road by Dr. Trent's house (lately McClellan's headquarters), came up to Magruder's troops.[6] Here he found Lee watching the enemy. After consultation, the two agreed that the evening was too far advanced for an effective movement and that Jackson should return to his bivouac and begin his march in pursuit at dawn the next morning. Scarcely had Jackson returned to the north bank of the river when a rapid outbreak of firing gave evidence that Magruder was attacking.

Magruder must have been thunderstruck with bewilderment near the close of the action about dark when Major Walter H. Taylor of Lee's staff handed him a message from the commanding general (evidently written before Lee decided to call off the attack without informing him): "I regret much that you have made so little progress today in pursuit of the enemy. In order to reap the fruits of our victory[,] the pursuit should be most vigorous. I must urge you, then, again to press on his rear rapidly and steadily. We must lose no more time or he will escape us entirely. . . . P.S.—Since the above was written[,] I learn from Major Taylor that you are under the impression that General Jackson has been ordered not to support you. On the contrary, he has been directed to do so, and to push the pursuit vigorously." Magruder wrote, " . . . I was uncertain whether General Jackson had obeyed his orders to go elsewhere or not . . ." In Magruder's front was an open field, beyond which the enemy occupied a series of heavy earthworks, hidden

by forest, and outnumbered his command about three to one.[7]
Lee had underestimated the strength of McClellan's rear
guard, which was able to continue its retreat during the night.

During Huger's absence, Mahone, his senior brigadier,
assumed command of the two brigades marching on the
Charles City Road. When the head of the column reached
Brightwell's farm, the advance guard encountered a small
party of enemy cavalry, which quickly disappeared. At this
point, the Poplar Springs Road passed from the Darbytown
Road north to Jordan's Ford and the New Road and continued
over White Oak Swamp to the Williamsburg Road. It was
known that Heintzelman's Federal corps had been encamped
in the area north of Mahone's present position and that
Brigadier General Philip Kearny's division had constituted
Heintzelman's left, closest to the Charles City Road. It was
anticipated that, by use of this crossing of the swamp or any
lower crossing, Kearny's division would attempt its retreat.
On meeting the cavalry scouts, Mahone deemed it essential to
the safety of his column, before leaving the Poplar Springs
Road, to learn if Kearny's division had left camp. With this
view, he immediately halted the column and dispatched a
reconnoitering party, which soon returned and reported the
enemy's column then in the act of crossing the swamp about
half a mile from the Confederate position.

Fearing that the lower crossings might be unduly clog-
ged with troops, Kearny had decided to pass his men on the
Poplar Springs Road. Mahone promptly placed his brigade in
position to meet the approach of this force, while Armistead's
brigade lay drawn up by the Poplar Springs Road as a reserve.[8]
In a few minutes, Kearny's advance guard crossed the double
arm of the swamp and collided with Mahone's skirmishers.
While fire was being exchanged, Huger arrived at the scene,
and of course, resumed command. Kearny, arriving and reconnoitering the ground about the same time, ordered a withdrawal to a lower crossing. Just after Kearny's men withdrew,
Huger sent two regiments of light troops into the woods to
more actively engage the enemy while he examined the country,
the map furnished him being worthless.

It appeared to Huger that the Federals had not retired
from their camps; and as his division was marching on the

Charles City Road, Kearny's was being left behind, an obvious danger. From captured soldiers and a boy who had been over the swamp with a message, he learned that there was a road, called the New Road, running along the edge of the swamp and that Kearny's main body was on the other side of the swamp. To prevent Kearny's division from marching into his own during the night, he ordered Captain Carey F. Grimes's battery of Mahone's brigade, supported by one of Wright's regiments, northward on the Poplar Springs Road and across the swamp to the intersection of that road with the New Road and Jordan's Ford. Armistead's brigade would remain along the Poplar Springs Road in ready support of this force until daylight.[9] At that time, Wright would proceed along Jordan's Ford and the New Road in order to send him word of the location of the enemy and to guard the left flank of the main force, which would resume the pursuit on Huger's assigned route.

The enemy withdrew after a sharp skirmish and the arrival of Grimes's battery. At that time, Mahone's force had captured fifteen soldiers. Just after the men began to bivouac a little farther down the Charles City Road, one of Kearny's aides, trying to communicate with his general, came trotting up the road with an escort of cavalry. The front troops of Mahone's brigade fired at the group and almost destroyed it. The aide and a few of the cavalrymen wheeled their horses around and escaped, leaving behind three men and three horses killed. The night was very dark, and a heavy rainstorm set in.

At early dawn, 30 June, Wright led his infantry across woods and fields, turned his van onto Jordan's Ford near Hobson's house, and proceeded southeast along the ford. Huger learned from him that Kearny's division had recrossed the swamp after the evening skirmish. This satisfied Huger that Kearny had changed his route of retreat from the Poplar Springs Road to the New Road. Hence, the next crossing which seemed to require the same precaution as with the Poplar Springs Road was Fisher's Ford, which was a better crossing than the first and was known to lead directly to a large enemy camp. Huger's main body continued the march at daylight, the column moving cautiously. The advance guard captured many prisoners and killed some couriers, one bearing a paper, which was handed to Huger. It was an order to Kearny directing him to retire and to keep a strong battery with his rear guard. This indicated to Huger that the enemy had not yet retired and could collide again with his left flank.

More soldiers were captured when the head of the column reached Fisher's Ford. The prisoners said that a considerable body of troops had passed from across the swamp to the Charles City Road the previous evening. This information satisfied Huger that Kearny's division was in front of his column. While the leading elements of his advance guard were crossing the bridge over Fisher's Ford, firing suddenly broke out from the enveloping woods. The Confederates pushed across the bridge and found the road blockaded by huge pine trees, which had been felled across it at that point in a great mass. Farther on were other obstructions of felled pines, the masses varying in size and extending on the road more than a mile.

Mahone, a distinguished engineer, found it best to cut a road around the obstructions. Evidently it was easier to chop down the few trees remaining than to clear the road. This would be the most efficient way for the artillery and wagons to continue the march. Huger sent word to Lee that his march was obstructed, and his engineer corps was sent to the left of the road to fell trees. For this work, the division was deficient in tools; hence, the column was delayed while the trees were being chopped down and dragged aside. A force of Huger's cavalry galloped back from the front, having been unsuccessful in an effort to draw the enemy into an ambush. Two of Mahone's regiments were deployed, one on either side of the main road, and advanced with fixed bayonets. While trees were being felled in the woods, skirmishing was kept up in front, the Federal soldiers readily yielding to the advance. D. H. Hill, with Jackson's command near White Oak Bridge, sent his engineer officer through the swamp to ask Huger if that officer's division could engage the enemy's main body in front. Huger explained his delay.

In the afternoon, when Huger's advance drove off the Federals, who were still felling trees, the head of the column entered a large open field on high ground, opposite the woods on the right of the road. This was Brackett's field, near P. Williams's house. Powerful, rifled artillery opened fire at the troops when they appeared. This was a very heavy and destructive fire; and a considerable number of Mahone's men, dreadfully wounded, were borne to the rear. Though the view was screened by a narrow belt of woods, the enemy could be seen in force about a mile down the road.

It was deemed necessary to reconnoiter the Federal position thoroughly before pushing farther. Captain Marcellus N. Moorman's battery of Mahone's brigade, followed soon after by Wright's reserve artillery under Lieutenant Colonel A. S. Cutts, advanced over the new road by the obstructions to test the Union position and force. Moorman's six cannons went into battery on Brackett's field, the advance guard of two regiments deploying in support. These guns opened a sharp fire, which was returned with great energy and effect.

Huger went to the front and examined the enemy's position. Cutts's seven guns arrived, but he did not order them into the duel. On the contrary, he withdrew four of Moorman's guns and kept up only a moderate fire. His artillery supports lay on the ground without making any movement, while the wounded were immediately withdrawn to the woods and treated. The sound of heavy firing could be heard about two miles to the right where Longstreet's command was engaged in furious battle.

About an hour before dark, Moorman's remaining guns, badly damaged, were withdrawn, while the Federal artillery still flamed. On the left, the main branch of the swamp, half a mile wide, approached very near. The right appeared to be firmer ground, and Huger determined to turn the enemy's artillery from his main body by moving a regiment of infantry to his right. His troops encamped while the Federals fired in a different direction from their bivouac. The fire did not cease until late at night.

On the day of the battle, a diarist wrote: "Once more all men are execrating Gen. Huger. It is alleged that he *again* failed to obey an order, and kept his division away from the position assigned it, which would have prevented the escape of McClellan. If this be so, who is responsible, after his alleged misconduct at the battle of the Seven Pines?" Virginia editors who had not given up the hope of seeing Huger ruined were again attacking him. The only reason the Federal army

escaped capture at White Oak Swamp, their newspapers claimed, was because he had disobeyed his orders by not sending his
division into action. He wrote: "As to an Editor sitting in his
office and scribbling about my movements, I cannot come out
and contradict him. The idea that one division, reduced to
some 6000 effectives[,] could capture an army of 100,000 is
simply ridiculous."[10]

Though the journalists' claim could not be realized, why
had Huger declined to attack, leaving Longstreet's command
to fight alone?

Longstreet's command had been placed in position
southwest of the Charles City Crossroads and was anxiously
awaiting the arrival of Huger's and Jackson's forces before
beginning the attack. During this time, the enemy opened with
artillery fire, which swept down the Long Bridge Road; and
Longstreet's skirmishers, advancing, engaged the Federal
pickets. It was about 3 o'clock when Huger's artillery opened
quite briskly. Thinking that this was the prearranged signal to
indicate that Huger's and Jackson's troops were in position,
Longstreet hurriedly ordered forward three or four batteries to
assure those commanders that his men were in position. As
soon as his first gun was discharged, the enemy opened a
tremendous fire from four six-gun batteries. The Federals being
in great force in his front, an engagement was brought on at
once, although it was not designed that this should be until the
troops on the left were in position to attack. The battle had
opened by accident.

Owing to the nature of the ground, concert of action
could not be attained. Longstreet's ground was much lower
than that occupied by the enemy and was greatly cut up by
ravines and covered with dense woods, tangled undergrowth,
streams, and marshes. As a result, his brigades struck the
enemy in piecemeal. Still he held A. P. Hill's division in
reserve, to be fresh for the pursuit after Jackson and Huger
joined battle. The opposing division under McCall was eventu-
ally driven from its position. But when McCall was reinforced
by three divisions, Longstreet found himself on the defensive.
Neither command on his left had come up. Couriers from
Huger arrived with word that the enemy was disputing his
passage of the swamp.[11] He therefore sent Hill's troops in to

relieve those on the battlefield, and it was with difficulty that the enemy's fierce counterblows were beaten off.

Owing to his inaccurate and incomplete map and the erroneous answers of guides, Lee believed previous to the battle that the Long Bridge Road was the route of McClellan's retreat. He also believed that the retreat had been arrested at the Charles City Crossroads, Longstreet's command blocking the route. He accordingly posted Holmes's division in Longstreet's rear at New Market Heights, covering the convergence of the roads there. After a personal and hazardous reconnaissance south of the Long Bridge Road, he discovered another road, which would better serve the purpose of the retreating foe. When Davis, meeting him returning from the reconnaissance, remonstrated with him on account of the exposure to which he had subjected himself, he replied that he could not get the required information otherwise and therefore had gone himself. The president could well understand. He was unable to find a guide with enough knowledge of the area to conduct him from one Confederate column to another. Holmes moved his division to the new position and waited for the Federals with their trains to pass. McClellan, however, had chosen the Willis Church Road, which offered a shorter and better route of escape, taking neither road pointed out by Lee.[12]

The clouds of dust from Holmes's marching column caused a heavy fire from the gunboats in the James to be directed at the troops, and portions of the cavalry and artillery broke and fled from the terrifying sounds of the exploding 10-inch shells. It had been reported that the Federals were retreating in considerable confusion on the road; but by the time Holmes's infantry was in position, they had taken the alarm and were drawn up in line of battle on the commanding heights of Malvern Hill. Due to the heavy growth of forest timber and dense underbrush, only five of the six guns Holmes intended to open at the enemy could be placed in battery. Before this could be accomplished, a devastating fire of field artillery was opened from the heights at the Confederates from some thirty guns so placed, which, with the aid of the gunboats, struck them in front and on both flanks simultaneously. The enemy's guns occupied such an extent of ground on Malvern Hill that it gave them almost a cross fire on Holmes's artillery, which, due to the great loss of men and horses, crippled his battery after about an hour's firing.

Holmes, junior only to Lee, reconnoitered personally. He observed that the ground would not admit of more guns being put in battery and noted also that an assault by his infantry would have required a march of over three quarters of a mile up a steep hill destitute of cover. He reported, "The strength of the enemy's position and their imposing numbers were such that to attempt an attack upon them with my small force unsupported would have been perfect madness. . . ."[13] Opposing Holmes's scant six thousand troops were three divisions and a portion of McClellan's reserve artillery.

Early that morning, Magruder, after a delay of confusion for want of guides, had proceeded with his command to the Darbytown Road to be held in reserve behind Longstreet's forces. About half past four that afternoon, he received an order from Longstreet, as second in command of the army (though both Holmes and Huger ranked him), to reinforce Holmes. The order was given under Lee's direction and was intended to cover Longstreet's rear in the event that the enemy should drive Holmes's division.[14] After putting his column in motion on the Darbytown Road, he met with Lieutenant Colonel R. H. Chilton, Lee's chief of staff, on the road near its junction with the Long Bridge Road. Chilton conducted him over a road through the woods, designating its intersection with the New Market Road as the point at which Magruder's right was to rest. Although the indicated area was completely exposed to the fire of the gunboats,[15] Chilton instructed him to form his command there and stated that, by marching his men diagonally through the woods, Magruder would thus find the position in which he would support Holmes. Under this vague and haphazard plan, the troops could easily become separated and lost in the thick woods and swamps. Accordingly, Magruder rode along the New Market Road in the hope of conferring with Holmes.

Failing to find him near sunset, Magruder directed Major Brent of his staff to search for Holmes and to ask if he had any suggestion concerning what position Magruder should take in order to give him a proper support. Then he rode to one of his brigades and ordered the commander to advance through the woods in obedience to Chilton's directions. The commander replied that it was impossible to do so without disorganizing his brigade, owing to the density of the woods and the approaching darkness. When Magruder told him that it was Lee's order through Chilton, he attempted to execute it but withdrew after losing a portion of his brigade and all but one of his staff officers. In the meantime, Magruder rode to hurry forward the remainder of his command, whose march was delayed by his mistaken guide.

Meanwhile, on finding Holmes's tent, Major Brent explained his mission and inquired if the division commander had any suggestion regarding what position Magruder should take to carry out his orders. Holmes, doubtless ashamed and angered at the portion of his command who had fled from the fire of the gunboats and disappointed at not having a fair opportunity to give battle, answered very brusquely that he had no suggestion to make. Brent then asked if he could tell him where the enemy was and in what probable force. "No," Holmes replied sharply. When the major said that he was returning to Magruder and would carry any message if Holmes desired to send one, he was again answered in the negative. "His bearing," Brent noted, "was the most singular I have ever seen, and was marked by the absence of even a simulation of ordinary courtesy. I left him in wonder, after having extracted from him four Nos as the sum total of my results."[16]

On another part of the field, Magruder received an order from Longstreet to bring one-half of his command to that officer's battlefield and an order from Chilton soon after to proceed with the whole of it to Longstreet. The command, arriving after the fight, relieved Longstreet's troops.

McClellan had gained much needed time from the feeble attack on his rear guard at Savage Station the day before. Instead of his marching columns being compelled to return to support the rear guard, his entire army had been able to cross White Oak Swamp, destroy all the bridges, and most effectively obstruct the roads and fords by felling heavy trees in and across them. On the morning of 30 June, he had posted one of his corps commanders, General Franklin, with three divisions to repel any attempt on the part of the Confederates to cross the swamp. Wherever possible, Franklin's artillery had been placed to take every advantage of the terrain. With the crests of hills serving as natural breastworks, the cannons, pointing just over the brows, were in a manner sheltered and the gun crews protected. In front the swampland was a wooded wilderness above a vast stagnant river, where the water was high and the surrounding countryside marshy from the severe thunderstorm during the night. At one end of the front, the smoldering, tangled ruins of White Oak Bridge, until recently the safest and best crossing, were commanded by some of these batteries and detachments of sharpshooters hidden in the swamp. On the north side of the swamp, the road for more than a quarter of a mile approached the bridge crossing through low ground, open to artillery fire from the Federal side. At the other end was posted an infantry regiment with a field gun, together with some three thousand troops sent out as pickets by Brigadier General Henry W. Slocum, whose division opposed Huger's. Of the disposition of his main body, Slocum reported, "The infantry necessary to support the artillery was posted on the flanks of the batteries, and the balance so disposed as to be entirely protected from the fire of the enemy's artillery."[17]

Jackson, with the largest command in the army, arrived in the vicinity of White Oak Bridge about noon. About quarter of two, twenty-eight pieces of his artillery opened suddenly, "the severity of which," Franklin wrote, "I had never heard equalled in the field."[18] The Federals abandoned their position on one side of the road in extreme haste and confusion. One of Jackson's batteries advanced nearer to the crossing to shell the sharpshooters from the woods, a working party was sent to repair the bridge, and cavalry forded the stream and advanced toward the position from which the enemy had been driven. But the Federals still held a position on the other side of the roadway; and the cavalrymen, artillerists, and bridge builders stampeded to the rear for cover. The men who had been laboring at the bridge refused to return. Meanwhile, Jackson's smoothbore guns turned in the new direction, at long range, which gave the enemy immense advantage with their rifled cannon. While Jackson's position was exposed to the enemy, the Union guns were entirely concealed from view. Not even the smoke from them could be seen.

Early in the afternoon, Wright reported to Jackson that

he had scouted along the New Road and had found the enemy's camps in the area north of the swamp abandoned, which revealed that McClellan's whole army had crossed. When he asked for orders, Jackson instructed him to move along the swamp and effect a crossing if possible, the enemy being in large force in his front and obstinately disputing a crossing at the destroyed bridge. Wright then recrossed the swamp on Brackett's Ford, driving back Federal pickets from the vicinity, and made a thorough reconnaissance before proceeding ahead:

> I ascertained that the road debouched from the swamp into an open field (meadow), commanded by a line of high hills, all in cultivation and free from timber. Upon this range of hills the enemy had posted heavy batteries of field artillery, strongly supported by infantry, which swept across the meadow by a direct and cross-fire, and which could be used with terrible effect upon my column while struggling through the fallen timber in the wood through the swamp.[19]

Wright doubtless sent word back to Jackson of the folly of attempting a crossing anywhere along the line of the swamp. In fact, he abandoned his intention of proceeding farther, withdrew his troops, and sought a crossing higher up the swamp to rejoin Huger.

Huger and Jackson, in communication with each other during the day, independently reconnoitered the front personally; and both felt that no crossing of the swamp should be attempted. If, however, Huger, Jackson's senior, had felt otherwise, he could have ordered an attack by the entire Confederate left, some twenty-four thousand troops. But he knew that, before reaching the Federal position, his own troops would have to march a mile in the enemy's view, stopping every few paces to load and fire and would have been unable to fire at all while struggling through the blockades and deep swampland under a terrific direct and cross fire of both musketry and superior artillery. Federal reinforcements, too, were in abundance. When the enemy merely spotted Wright's skirmishers on Brackett's Ford, two brigades of an idle division and a battery of reserve artillery were rushed to Slocum to assist in opposing their passage. (In contrast, Magruder's command had been moved from Jackson's proximity; and J. G. Walker's brigade, four thousand strong and the largest brigade in the army, had been rerouted from the support of Huger's division to that of Holmes.) Huger wrote, "If he [McClellan] could have been caught[,] it would have been a very pretty thing," but as "much as it may be regretted, it could not be helped."[20]

A nightmare of hell was suffered by Colonel Micah Jenkins, who commanded the brigade that spearheaded Longstreet's attack. His bridle reins were shot in two near his hand, a hole was shot through his saddle blanket, and a musket ball and piece of shell tore fifteen holes through an India-rubber overcoat rolled and tied on behind his saddle. His sword was shot off at the point and the knob and was half in two near the hilt. His horse was hit in two places, while he was wounded on the shoulder by a grapeshot and was struck on the chest and leg by shell fragments. At times while he was riding up and down the line, his men would turn their heads and give him a look as if to say, We can go no farther, then he would wave his hand to them and they would charge again. At one time, when he saw how fast his men were falling around him, he stopped and prayed to God to send a bullet through his heart. He was seen coming out of the battle weeping like a child at the destruction of his brave, noble men.[21]

At Chapultepec Huger had acted against both orders and odds by opening the fire of his heavy artillery over the heads of the American stormers, risking all to prevent Scott's attacking masses from being defeated if not annihilated and the army itself from being trapped and destroyed in the Valley of Mexico. His object before the Halls of Montezuma and his object at White Oak Swamp were the same—to save lives.

7. *Malvern Hill: The Enemy Escapes*

The result of the Battle of White Oak Swamp was McClellan's success in protecting his trains from rear and flank attack as they passed on the Willis Church Road en route to Harrison's Landing, near Westover. The purpose of the Federal commander was to gather his army at that point by the James where the greater width and depth of the river would enable Goldsborough's fleet to approach him with ease and maneuver for his defense.

Lee met with Longstreet, A. P. Hill, and Magruder on the Long Bridge Road at an early hour the next morning, 1 July. The generals discussed yesterday's battle, being then on the battlefield. Later, when a brigadier reported to Lee for orders and expressed his anxiety that McClellan might escape, the commanding general exploded, "Yes, he will get away because I cannot have my orders carried out."[1] His latest strategy had been completely frustrated. But the Federals were not yet beyond reach, and he was determined to strike again before they escaped entirely. Feeling exhausted and unwell, he asked Longstreet to remain at his side so that the latter could take command of the army should the need arise. Jackson joined the group, and the generals conferred for some time. Then they rode near Willis Church, where they met D. H. Hill, who repeated a grim description of Malvern Hill which he had obtained from an army chaplain who had been raised in the neighborhood. Malvern Hill was the position Holmes had declined to attack, deeming the act "perfect madness." Satisfied that a battle there could only be fatal, Hill advised, "If General McClellan is there in force, we had better let him alone." Longstreet laughed; then he said, "Don't get scared, now that we have got him whipped."[2]

Late in the evening on 30 June, Huger made Fisher's house his headquarters and issued orders for Mahone to push pickets forward and to advance as soon as the Charles City Road was clear, the remainder of the division to follow. At a very early hour this morning, he was ready to continue the pursuit when Mahone informed him that the enemy's pickets still covered the front, which indicated that Slocum's main body had not yet retired. Countermanding his previous orders, he directed Armistead, with his own and Wright's brigades, to march on a road to the right so as to take the enemy in flank. This movement would clear his front and allow the continuance of his advance. At 3 A.M. he watched Armistead's brigade clear the adjacent road and Wright's brigade follow, though their progress through the woods was slow.

When Huger received notice from Longstreet that the Charles City Road was clear, he was much disappointed that Mahone had not discovered the retreat. Franklin's troops, too, had marched unnoticed by Longstreet during the night, passing within easy range of the latter's artillery.[3] So if there was no main body in front, why were pickets still posted? When Huger advanced with Mahone's and Ransom's brigades, the pickets gave themselves up as prisoners and said that the army had retired without ordering them in.

Unfortunately, Armistead misunderstood the purpose of Huger's countermanding orders and kept following the blind road. A march of two or three miles brought him to the Long Bridge Road, where he halted the column. There he reported to Lee, who directed him to proceed to the Quaker Road. Moving through the woods around Carter's (later Garthright's) farm, he met with Major T. M. R. Talcott, formerly Huger's chief engineer at Norfolk and now serving as an aide-de-camp to Lee.

Talcott told him that the enemy was near, and the column took position.

Huger meanwhile pushed on as rapidly as he could with his remaining brigades, believing that the other two, finding the front clear, would come up in the rear. Federal knapsacks, blankets, camp equipment, and rifles that had been thrown down or broken by striking the butts against trees were scattered along the route of his advance. As the troops passed the battlefield of the day before, they saw dead and wounded soldiers, scattered accouterments, including some breastplates, and a battery of captured guns. Huger halted the column on reaching the Charles City Crossroads. The column was delayed here as Howell Cobb's brigade of Magruder's forces and Jackson's command moved along the Willis Church Road. Couriers had been sent in the night to Huger and Jackson with instructions to hasten their march, but no directive had been given since. Which road should the division take? Was it Lee's intention to crowd all his troops on the Willis Church Road? Finally, Major Taylor, one of Lee's aides, arrived and conducted the column on the Willis Church Road, reaching the front before noon. When Huger reported to Lee at this time, he learned that Armistead's and Wright's brigades had been posted on the front line by Lee's order.

Lee gave verbal orders for immediate attack by Jackson, Magruder, and Huger. Jackson's command was to take position on the left facing Malvern Hill, Magruder's on the immediate right of Jackson's. Magruder was directed to march on the Quaker Road to reach his position. Having seen Lee's map, Longstreet expressed some doubt as to the road in question being the Quaker Road. Magruder then interrogated his three guides separately. Satisfied that they were right, he told Longstreet that, if the latter would give him an order to march by any other road, he would obey it with pleasure. This Longstreet declined to do, being as unfamiliar with the country as his junior. After proceeding from the Long Bridge Road for about a mile and a half, Magruder halted his command and seemed much perplexed. He had passed the position his command was to occupy, had flanked Malvern Hill, and was now headed toward the James. Again he questioned his guides closely. Was this the Quaker Road or was there any other road in the area known as the Quaker? The guides, who had lived many years in the neighborhood, were positive in their declaration that this was the only Quaker Road known to them. Magruder said that there must be some mistake, as his order was to advance on the Quaker Road and take a position for battle but that this road was evidently leading him away from his assigned position. He therefore would not advance farther on it. At the same moment, he was overtaken by Longstreet, to whom he explained his trouble. When Longstreet expressed his desire that the troops should return to another road parallel to this one but nearer to Jackson's right, Magruder repeated his request for an order to move back. Though Longstreet said that he could not give the order, he proposed to notify Lee of the problem. Lieutenant Colonel Chilton of Lee's staff arrived about this time with an order for Magruder to move to the road to which Longstreet had referred, and the line of march was reversed and headed in that direction. But Magruder had, in fact, been on the only Quaker Road, although the Willis Church Road was called Quaker by some. The confusion caused by the two roads delayed the troops two or three hours, during which time Armistead's column formed on Jackson's right and occupied part of the ground assigned to Magruder.

D. H. Hill had not exaggerated the great natural strength of Malvern Hill. There tier after tier of batteries rose toward the crest in the form of an amphitheater and were supported by powerful lines of infantry, sheltered by fences, ditches, ravines, and hastily constructed entrenchments. If the first line were carried, another and another still more difficult remained in the rear. Immediately in front the ground was open, varying in width from a quarter to half a mile, sloping gradually from the crest, and was completely swept by a cross fire of artillery and musketry. To reach the open ground, the Confederates would have to advance through a broken and thickly wooded country traversed nearly throughout its whole extent by a swamp passable at few places and difficult at those. The whole was in range of the light and heavy batteries on the heights and gunboats in the river.

Lee directed Longstreet to reconnoiter the enemy's left and to report if a frontal attack would be feasible. The Confederate right appeared to offer a position for sixty guns, while the open ground along Jackson's front appeared to be suitable for concentrating at least a hundred cannons. Longstreet believed that a heavy cross fire from these guns on those of the enemy would throw the latter into disorder and thus permit a simultaneous infantry assault. He so reported; and in the early afternoon, Lee ordered disposition accordingly, sending an engineer corps to cut a road for the proposed batteries on the right and issuing an order to division commanders: "Batteries have been established to rake the enemy's lines. If it is broken, as is probable, Armistead, who can witness the effect of the fire, has been ordered to charge with a yell. Do the same."⁴ But the order was written in anticipation of the establishment of such batteries. Lee's chief of artillery could find no site from which his heavy guns could play on the enemy without endangering the Confederate troops in front, and the nature of the ground afforded no area for proper concentration of the reserve artillery.

It was just after 3 o'clock when Lee deemed it impracticable to make the assault from the front and rode with Longstreet to the left to determine if McClellan's extreme right could be outflanked and attacked. After a hasty reconnaissance, he ordered Longstreet to move his command into position to begin the assault. As the column commenced the march, however, he concluded that it was too late to make the movement.⁵ While the troops were returning to their former position about 6 o'clock, a terrible fire in front was heard. Neither Lee nor Longstreet knew the cause, but the battle had opened.

Like yesterday's battle, this one opened by mistake. Earlier in the day, Armistead, then the senior officer at the front, called for artillery and ordered his skirmish line to drive back the enemy's pickets far enough to enable the guns to be placed in position. Only one of the four batteries that arrived could be placed at a time. Captain C. F. Grimes's battery of Mahone's brigade, the first to reach the front, arrived about 3 o'clock; but only its two rifled cannons were of sufficient range. Federal artillery, which had been firing at intervals into the woods concealing the Confederates, now opened so hot and rapid a fire that Grimes's guns could scarcely get into action before they were knocked to pieces. Huger's chief of artillery observed that the two guns were opposed by the simultaneous fire of six six-gun batteries.[6]

While Grimes's gun crews and nearly all of his artillery horses were falling in the storm of exploding shells, a heavy body of Federal sharpshooters was approaching to reinforce the pickets opposing the Confederate skirmish line. With the object of repelling the enemy, Armistead ordered Wright's brigade and the bulk of his own to charge. The troops rushed forward exposed and excited. While officers of some of the charging regiments were successful in preventing their men from advancing farther than necessary, others, urging their men onward, believed that they were to charge the enemy's main position! These troops soon found themselves pinned down under cover of the ravine nearest McClellan's forces.

Under conditions that forbade hope and invited disaster, Lee had failed to rescind the order for the frontal attack. D. H. Hill, hearing the troops yelling on the right, took this as the appointed signal, moved the irregular line of his division out of the woods, and charged the Union front alone. Suffering heavy losses under the enemy's concentrated fire, he sent to Jackson for reinforcements. Jackson ordered forward his own division and most of Ewell's; but owing to the difficulty of the ground and the increasing darkness of the night, they arrived too late to render assistance.

After Hill's division was repulsed from the field about sunset, Magruder received for the first time a copy of Lee's unrescinded order.[7] This he naturally accepted as current, but none of his troops were in position to execute it. While he was engaged in hurrying the men to the edge of the woods, Lee received reports that the enemy's troops and trains were falling back from Malvern Hill and that Armistead's minor skirmish was successful. A reconnaissance, however, would have proven both reports erroneous. Too impatient to take this precaution and believing that the enemy was about to escape him, Lee hastened to send an order to Magruder through one of Magruder's staff officers: "General Lee expects you to advance rapidly. He says it is reported the enemy is getting off. Press forward your whole line and follow up Armistead's successes."[8] Magruder had expressly said again and again during the day

that he did not want to order a charge until the artillery had
played on the crowded ranks that lined the opposite heights,[9]
but now he was required to obey Lee's orders. His brigades
were scattered over a wide front, and like Hill's, went in
piecemeal. Fire from bewildered brigades in the rear added to
the casualties of those in front and increased the confusion. At
these attacks, the enemy's artillery fire, which had been heavy,
became inexpressibly furious. Immediately Magruder called to
Lee and Longstreet for reinforcements. Longstreet's command
advanced; but like the reinforcements sent by Jackson on the
left, it reached the battlefield too late. The five batteries
posted in front of Jackson's left had been as quickly overpowered as the artillery in Armistead's front. The force of the
Confederate onset died away because the artillery was ineffec-
tive and the infantry attacks were uncoordinated. Furthermore,
there was a gap nearly a mile wide between the forces on the
left and those on the right.

The gap resulted from a combination of causes. With
Armistead's troops on part of Magruder's assigned ground
and the brigadier being charged with commencing the attack,
Lee had decided to change the arrangement of his front.
Huger's division was to form the center, with Jackson remain-
ing on the left and Magruder taking post on the right of Huger.

Magruder sent Major Brent of his staff about 3 o'clock
to find Huger in order to learn where Huger's right would connect with his left and where Huger's left would join Jackson's
right. Brent immediately rode to the left and searched in vain
for Huger's division. Then riding to the rear, where he
discovered Ransom's brigade, he found Huger on the side of
the road leading into Carter's farm. He remembered, "I had
several times met Genl. Huger, and found him a courteous
gentleman." After stating his mission, he asked the division
commander exactly where his line of battle on the right would
terminate. Huger replied that he had not been to the front and
could not give the information sought and then added with
strong feeling, "I do not know where my brigades are, and I
hear that at least some of them have been moved without my
knowledge by orders independent of me, and I have no information enabling me to answer to your inquiries." "But
General," Brent replied, "General Magruder has received his

orders from General Lee, and they indicate that you are to fill the gap between him and General Jackson; and can you not give me some indication at least where your line will join with General Jackson?" Huger answered that he could not, as the control of his division had been taken from him.[10]

Since Lee had shown Huger in the morning where the two brigades under Armistead were located and because Huger's other two brigades early in the afternoon had left the Willis Church Road and been posted in line of battle by the division commander's orders, Huger did know where his brigades were. In his statement to Brent, he evidently meant that he did not know whose assigned position they were occupying, not yet having been to the front. Nor had he at this time received official notification that his division was to occupy the center.[11] Unaware of the earlier misunderstanding between himself and Armistead, he believed that Lee had changed the line of march of Armistead's column from its intended course back to the Charles City Road without notifying him. If he had received the order for the frontal attack by this time, he knew that the commanding general was still controlling Armistead, who was to decide when to begin the attack. Communications passed between Lee and Armistead directly and independently of Huger. The division commander wondered if his presence on the field would again be ignored as it had been at Seven Pines. In this respect, he viewed Magruder's staff officer as a warning. After Brent left, he sent orders to Mahone and Ransom not to obey any orders which did not pass through his hands. This was to prevent any major general other than himself from taking control of his remaining brigades while he was present on the field.

When Brent returned to his commander, Magruder, much perplexed with the major's report, asked him to use all his efforts to advance Ransom's brigade to the front line. Brent reached Ransom about 5 o'clock and gave him Magruder's message. Ransom answered that he would be happy to comply with the request but that he was restrained by Huger's recent orders. When the brigade commander sent word to Huger for instructions, the reply sustained his action.

Brent had scarcely reported to Magruder when his commander directed him to again return and tell Ransom that he must bring up his troops and that to stand idle under the circumstances would expose him to the severest criticisms. Brent rode off and found Mahone's brigade between Ransom's and the front. He renewed Magruder's request to Ransom and supported it the best he could. Ransom said that his orders were peremptory and that he had to obey them. Brent then tried in vain to persuade Mahone to move his brigade forward. By the time he rejoined his commander, Magruder had received the order for the frontal attack. He told Brent to return again and not to leave Mahone and Ransom until he had persuaded at least one of them to move to the front.

Meanwhile, Magruder sent a communication directly to Ransom asking information about a battery reported to be near the brigade and requesting that the battery and the brigade report to him. When the message arrived about 5:45 P.M., Huger was with the brigade; and under his dictation, Ransom informed Magruder that neither he nor Huger knew where the battery on their left was and that any order to officers or men in Huger's division must be directed to the division commander.

When Magruder's plea for reinforcements reached army headquarters, Lee's chief of staff replied, "No troops to reenforce you with unless Huger's division has not been in, [in] which case you will call upon him to ascertain his position," adding that the brigades with Huger were to take position on Armistead's left.[12] But Magruder had already failed to obtain from Huger information regarding that officer's position. Further communication with Lee's headquarters resulted in an order:

> *July 1, 1862*
> *General Huger:*
> *The major-general [Magruder] desires that you will immediately put [that portion of] your division which was not engaged on Armistead's left, as Magruder requires re-enforcements.*
> *By order [of] General Lee:*
> *R. H. Chilton,*
> *Assistant Adjutant-General*[13]

Huger must have been outraged by the order, which he doubtless interpreted as a directive to relinquish the command of his division to Magruder in the form of reinforcements. One of his immediate subordinates had begun the engagement independently of his control, and now a junior was directing the battle. In the general atmosphere of ignorance and confusion, he disregarded the order. Apparently about this time, however, he was directed by Lee to send Mahone's brigade to support Cobb's of Magruder's division. When Mahone reached the front with his brigade, he reported to Magruder, who ordered him to support Wright's brigade. Then, Mahone recalled years later, "We went in with beautiful heroism and got butchered."[14]

In Magruder's second order to attack (to press forward his whole line), he was informed by Lee, "Ransom's brigade has gone on to re-enforce General Cobb." Like the first statement of Lee's first order (that Confederate batteries had been established), this one in his second was written in anticipation of the act. Aware that Ransom's brigade had not moved, Magruder, about 7 o'clock, sent word to the brigadier that he must have aid if only a regiment. The message was so pressing that Ransom dispatched one of his regiments to report to Magruder, and at the same time, sent an aide to Huger for orders. The aide returned from his completely frustrated division commander with somewhat discretionary instructions—to go or not but not to place himself under Magruder. Ransom immediately advanced with his remaining regiments through the woods, now darkened by twilight. As each of the first three reached the field, they were at once thrown into action by Magruder's orders. When Huger arrived at the front, he found that all his brigades were then under Magruder's immediate command. "As I was treated in the same manner at Seven Pines," he reported later, "I can only hope this course was accidental and required by the necessities of the service."[15]

Toward the close of the action, Lee, thinking that Magruder's forces were tending too far to the left, sent an order to the commander to press the enemy on his right. This lengthened the gap in the Confederate line, enabling the enemy to deliver, in addition to a front fire, a quarter enfilading fire from the otherwise idle troops facing the widened gap. At least three charges were made on that part of the field, and the southern dead lay almost in heaps.[16]

Lee found Magruder after the battle. Oblivious of his first order of the day, he asked Magruder why the latter had attacked. He was answered without hesitation, "In obedience to your orders, twice repeated."[17]

The result of Lee's gross mismanagement was the defeat and the disorganization of his entire army. A brigadier wrote, "The next morning by dawn I went off to ask for orders, when I found the whole army in the utmost disorder—thousands of straggling men asking every passer-by for their regiments; ambulances, wagons, and artillery obstructing every road, and together, in a drenching rain, presenting a scene of the most woeful and disheartening confusion."[18]

Under Huger's orders, his division was occupied in removing the wounded and burying the dead, who numbered just under five and a half thousand on the Confederate side. His ambulance details passed to the front and mingled freely with those of the enemy. A tacit truce seemed to prevail for some time. At length McClellan's rear guard was seen retiring slowly from view.

Lee ordered the pursuit continued. Longstreet's command, followed by Jackson's (with the exception of D. H. Hill's shattered division), moved on the New Market Road two miles through a heavy rainstorm, only to find that the enemy had obstructed the route. On 3 July, Lee directed Longstreet to countermarch to the Charles City Crossroads and move on Evelington Heights, which completely commanded McClellan's encampment, while Jackson was to reach the heights by taking the road to Westover. Longstreet was led by his guide away from his proper route and moved east instead of south. Jackson likewise missed his road and marched only three miles. The soldier assigned to him as a guide made a dreadfully stupid report and at length admitted that he knew nothing about the road to Westover. Meanwhile, Stuart's cavalry secured and held the heights for five hours, when, finding that the infantry was still six or seven miles distant and being pressed by the enemy's infantry, the commander was compelled to withdraw his troopers. The next day Lee saw the heights already fortified, with the front guarded by the gunboats, each side flanked by a creek, and approached by only one road. The position was even stronger than Malvern Hill. This ended the campaign, the Confederates withdrew nearer to Richmond on 8 July, and a month later McClellan's army was withdrawn to the North.

In the meantime, when one of Huger's generals sent him word that the records of the relative ranks of general officers had been returned to the adjutant general's office, he rode into Richmond, where he had the necessary books produced and an official list prepared. He immediately sent the list to Longstreet and called his attention to that officer's claim of seniority. Longstreet apologized, made a lame statement, and added a lie—that his impression had been confirmed by Assistant Secretary of War Albert T. Bledsoe, who, according to Longstreet, had told him that he was Huger's senior.[19]

8. The Banishment

Lee was responsible for the failure of every major battle of the Seven Days. He made no use of his staff to coordinate the attacks at Mechanicsville and White Oak Swamp. His offensive plan at Gaines' Mill failed because Stuart's ride around the Federal army had caused McClellan to change his base of supply, and consequently, Porter did not shift his troops as Lee had expected. Lee wrecked his strategy of 30 June by not anticipating the destruction of Grapevine Bridge by the retreating enemy, not vigorously attacking the Union rear guard at Savage Station as planned, underestimating the obstacle presented by White Oak Swamp, and miscalculating the Federal route of retreat from the swamp. When the Confederate guns failed to disorder the Federal batteries at Malvern Hill, he neglected to countermand his order for the frontal attack. From that moment, his control of the army was lost. Instead of utilizing his staff to insure concert of action in the execution of his strategies, he left the coordination of his principal commands to their commanders, whom he compelled to operate in a wooded, swampy country of confusing roads without any acquaintance of the ground. Confederate maps were inaccurate, incomplete, and difficult to understand. Though Lee had been a distinguished engineer, had resided in Richmond as commander in chief of the Virginia forces and then as military advisor to the president, and had been aware of the enemy's design to capture the capital, he had done nothing to procure reliable maps of the suburbs of his threatened city. Instead, he depended almost exclusively on guides, soldiers who knew little more than the way from their homes to Richmond. The invaders, on the other hand, knew their adversary's territory thoroughly, having prepared detailed maps.[1]

Lee never bore the repercussions for his blunders. Criticism was directed at innocent subordinates. Throughout the campaign, the army had spoken bitterly of Huger's "slowness." The troops and press viewed him as an easygoing, do-nothing general. It was said that McClellan's right while north of the Chickahominy had escaped destruction because Jackson had been too late in reaching the battlefield. The valley commander was returned to detached duty with a command reduced from four to its original two divisions. Magruder was blamed for the failure at Savage Station and was harshly criticized for the confusion and disaster at Malvern Hill. By previous arrangement, he was relieved of command and sent to the Trans-Mississippi Department. Holmes was much criticized for not having committed his division at White Oak Swamp and Malvern Hill. But his men owed him their lives.

Although Lee's attempts to destroy McClellan's army had failed miserably, the siege of the capital had been lifted. When someone congratulated Lee on his success, he replied that the congratulations were not due him but to the brave officers and men under him. "Longstreet," he said, "was the staff in my right hand."[2]

Lee more than fulfilled Longstreet's desire to become second in command of the army. He made immediate dispositions to rid not only the army but the whole state of those who ranked his favorite officer, that Longstreet would be next in command to him in Virginia.[3] Johnston, when he recovered from the wounds received at Seven Pines, would be sent to the West. G. W. Smith, yet on sick leave, was relieved of command. Holmes was sent to the Trans-Mississippi Department. Huger was relieved of command and named inspector of artillery and ordnance for the Confederacy, an empty title. To Longstreet, when Lee reorganized his forces, went the bulk of the army—in the aggregate over fifty thousand troops. That officer, through his manipulation of men and events, became the senior lieutenant general in the Confederate States when the rank was adopted in October 1862.

In retrospect of her brother's life, Lizzie Huger noted emphatically, "Genl Lee failed in friendship."⁴ Lee and Huger had served together at Fort Monroe and in Mexico; and for many years, the affection between them was almost brotherly. Lee was known to the Huger family as "Uncle Robert," and he called Mrs. Huger "beautiful little madam." The situation changed suddenly, however, when Huger became the talk of the army for the southern failure at Seven Pines. Lee believed the rumor in spite of their long friendship.⁵ This would account for his having included Longstreet in his offensive plans north of the Chickahominy, while having left Huger in the less demanding role of defense. He held Huger alone responsible for the wreck of his strategy of 30 June. In preparing his report in March 1863, he distinguished delicately between the inability of Huger and Jackson to cross White Oak Swamp: "not coming up," he complained of Huger, while Jackson had been "unable" to cross. Yet he stated two years before his death that he never did understand the reason for the delay.⁶ In addition, he expressed no dissatisfaction to Huger concerning the battles, gave him no opportunity to defend himself, and exiled him to a nonexistent job.

When the army withdrew from Malvern Hill, Huger marched the remnants of his division to the south side of the James, crossing on a pontoon bridge not far from Drewry's Bluff, and encamped near Falling Creek. By 28 July, he had restored his division to fighting condition, turned the command over to R. H. Anderson—Longstreet's choice—and was given a week's leave, his first since the war began. By now, his once brilliant reputation had been ruined. He warned his brother Cle, "You must expect to see me attacked in every way."⁷ Stories multiplied from his alleged failures contended that he was a chronic alcoholic and that he was always drunk when duty called, that his provisional grade of major general had been abated and that he had been assigned to duty with only his rank of colonel in the Confederate army. Some were even accusing him of treason. It was rumored, even among South Carolinians, that his wife was sister of Mrs. Wool, wife of the Union general in command of Fort Monroe. Some asserted that he was related to McClellan and that his "failures" had been made for his "relative's" benefit.

Again, too, he was viciously attacked in Congress, particularly by Wise's friend Representative Foote. Foote claimed that, if Huger had done his duty, McClellan's army would have been annihilated, thousands of patriotic lives been saved, the war most likely brought to an end, and southern independence been recognized. General Huger, he said, had been too slow; he had been so slow to join the Confederacy that his friends in South Carolina had hung their heads. Foote raved that there was enough evidence against Huger to convict a thousand criminals, that Rome had its Cataline, the American colonies their Benedict Arnold, and the Confederacy its Huger.[8]

When Huger offered to resign if this were desired of him, War Secretary Randolph begged him not to leave the service and told him of his value to the Confederacy. President Davis later told him that he especially desired his services in the West, where his vast experience could be most valuable in setting up much needed ordnance establishments in Texas.

As neither Lee nor the administration had verbally censured him, Huger doubtless felt that no detailed explanation in his report of the Seven Days was necessary. He directed his efforts instead to vindicating himself to the public. He applied to Randolph in mid-July, "As there is a very general impression among the people that I deserted Norfolk, and gentlemen who have traveled in the cars mention that they hear me thus spoken of continually, it seems to me, as nobody else will arrest the error, it is due to me that I should be allowed to publish the orders under which I acted."[9] At the same time, he made application to the War Department for copies of Johnston's and Longstreet's Seven Pines reports. As soon as he received the first, he pointed out the errors in it and asked Johnston's correction of them. When Johnston declined and did his best to discourage investigation, Huger requested Davis to grant him a court-martial. If this could not be done, he asked that a court of inquiry be assembled.[10]

During this time, Huger received a letter from Tattnall, who had been severely criticized for the destruction of the *Virginia*. At the naval officer's own request, a court of inquiry had been called concerning the public accusation. When censured by the court in June, he had demanded a court-martial, which had acquitted him in July. Huger's reply read:

Richmond   Sept'. 2nd 1862

My dear Comm^e.

I am much obliged to you for your letter of 28th ulto. The remarks of the Court of Enquiry were not justified by the facts or by the evidence you gave, of which you send an extract. As every body else has been making false statements concerning me, I suppose the Court thought they might safely do the same.
I had notice of the landing of the enemy at Ocean View before daylight on 10th May and immediately sent an orderly with the information to Capt Lee, and as I saw the [tugboat] Harmony in motion soon after, I thought she had been sent to you with the message I sent Capt Lee—that as my troops had been withdrawn & ammunition sent away[,] I could not defend [Norfolk] & would have to evacuate the place at once. If I had not been confident [that] Capt Lee had communicated with you[,] I would have sent about to inform you of the fact; but agree with you that it could make no difference whatever in the fate of the Virginia whether you knew the fact a few hours sooner or later.
I believe now [that] the destruction of the Va. was the salvation of Richmond. It woke them up & they went to work at the obstructions and batteries at Drewry's Bluff.
It has been my fate to be abused and [my] every act perverted. Falsehoods are manufactured against me at every street corner, and Ruffians in Congress under the protection of its Halls abuse me in the grossest manner. But I have devoted all my time & the little ability God has given me to the service of my country; and I trust that "truth is mighty & will prevail."
I do not fear the result. Like yourself[,] I have been unfortunate—but I believe [that] I can show[,] as

you have done, that I did the best I could under the
circumstances. Mrs H. & family are at Amelia
Springs or they would send much regards.

Very truly yours,
Benj. Huger[11]

Comm*e*. *Josiah Tattnall.*
Savannah Ga

By Davis's order, in answer to Huger's request for a
court-martial, Johnston was to put his statement in the form
of charges and specifications against Huger, or should he
decline, a court of inquiry would be assembled as soon as the
state of the public service would permit it. Johnston replied
that he was unable to draw up formal charges, insisting that he
could not contradict Longstreet's report as he had no evidence
against it, and added audaciously, "The passage in my report
of which he [Huger] complains was written to show that the
delay in commencing the action of May 31 was not by my
fault."[12] With this, Huger renewed his request for court[13] but
was soon after ordered on a tour of ordnance establishments,
arriving in Columbia, South Carolina, in November. Hearing
after his arrival in Columbia that Johnston had reported for
duty at the War Department, he asked that the court be
assembled before that officer was assigned to any distant
command.[14] He was answered that the state of the service
would not permit the granting of his request, and Johnston left
Richmond to take command of the Department of the West.

At the end of February 1863, Huger began an inspection
of the artillery and ordnance stores at Charleston and Savannah.
He received orders the following month to make a similar tour
through Lieutenant General E. Kirby Smith's Trans-Mississippi
Department. His son Frank wrote to him at this time:

I regret so much that you have to go West before you
get your court. It has set me to thinking if it could not be
avoided and one thing has suggested itself, that is, that
as your business will require time and research, could
you not apply for at least two or three competent persons as your aides and send them ahead to examine and
report on localities etc. and that would at least save a

great deal of labour for you and in the meantime write to
Mr. Davis and tell him in the plainest language that
you've now waited nearly a year for an opportunity to
refute officially a charge against yourself, affecting your
reputation as a soldier, dearer to you and your children
than all the world besides, that if you await your return
from the West [,] you can not possibly have the opportunity you desire till the fall and that you are not willing
to delay that long. Johnston is doing nothing now, and
the few witnesses you desire could be spared even during
active operations, and that you demand an immediate
investigation. You may depend on it that they will never
allow you a hearing as long as you leave their [con-
science?] alone. G. W. Smith I believe is aware that
Longstreet knew you ranked him, and I think moreover
that he knows something concerning some of the movements at Seven Pines in which Longstreet failed to
comply and that he used you to escape.[15] Longstreet is a
politician and nothing else, and I would like him to be
shewn up. As soon as you have cleared up that matter, I
hope you'll apply for active service . . .[16]

Huger wrote in reply:

I have written a letter to [the] Secy of War stating [that]
the Presdt. had authorized a Ct of Enquiry as soon as
the "Exigencies of the Service" would permit; and
stating [that] I claimed that Court even if the "Exigencies" deferred it for years. I have an answer that the letter has been declined by Col Gorgas [one of Huger's
lieutenants in Mexico and now the Confederacy's chief
of ordnance]. I may write again before I go [West] next
week, but as I am especially desired by the *Presdt* to go
on this duty, I do not see [that] I can decline going[,]
now [that] I have the order. . . . I do not know suitable
persons here to appoint [aides], & think [that] I will wait
till I get out to the Trans-Miss. Dept.[17]

After reporting at General Kirby Smith's headquarters
at Alexandria, Louisiana, Huger made a thorough inspection
through part of Texas of the various plants for manufacturing

ordnance supplies with the view of establishing foundries and arsenals. For this purpose, Josiah Gorgas had given him authority to draw from the Treasury in Richmond to the amount of one and a half million dollars. But with the fall of Vicksburg and Port Hudson, the enemy gained control of the Mississippi River; and the Trans-Mississippi region was in great measure isolated from the rest of the Confederacy. Without communication with Richmond, Huger was without funds.

Huger's orders from Richmond had not assigned him to Smith's department. The department's funds were controlled by Smith's chief of ordnance and artillery, who declined to relinquish any control to Huger. Smith had independently named Huger chief of the bureau of ordnance; but the authority of this office, headed by Captain Benjamin Huger, Jr., did not exceed the mere storing of returns from the different ordnance establishments and commanders in the field, to be transmitted to Richmond for settlement at the Treasury if and when communication would be reopened. The iron works, the niter and mining bureau, and the San Antonio Arsenal were also under Huger's charge. But as each establishment had its own commanding officer, he could render service only in a general supervisory capacity. Hopefully awaiting further orders from the War Department placing him in position officially, he informed his wife, "I am better here with a nominal position than at Richd with no position at all."[18]

In June 1864, Huger's position in the Trans-Mississippi Department was officially defined. With the surrender of the Confederate forces a year later, he quietly entered civilian life.

Huger had crossed the Mississippi River with the intention of renewing his application for court on return to the East. But not until after the war was he able to recross the river.

9. *The Final Ruin*

There was no hope for official vindication in the defeated South. With its military courts no longer in existence, the South was convulsed for many years by postwar controversies, which were often caustic and undignified. Huger wanted no part of them. He explained to an inquiring friend: "If our cause had been successful, I should have insisted upon the investigation which was due me; but, when we surrendered, I determined [that] it was no time to redress private wrongs; that I must continue to bear them ... I would make no public statement now [during the reconstruction period] ..."[1] He added that he could only "trust to time and truth" for his vindication.[2]

Huger would not return to South Carolina while its government was in alien hands. In January 1866, soon after settling in Baltimore with his wife, he accepted a position as a trustee for an iron company in New York City, and within three months, became its president.

Mrs. Huger's health became seriously impaired in the summer of 1867. By fall, she was completely bedridden. In late September, Huger penciled in his diary, "Oh, God[,] I have no hope but in thee!!" His wife died in early October; Ben, Jr., had died within the same week, the result of a liver ailment. Mrs. Huger's funeral services were held at Saint Paul's Episcopal Church, where the services of their son had been held only a few days before. Mother and son were buried together in Green Mount Cemetery.[3]

In January of 1869 Huger moved southward to a large farm called Gordonsdale in Fauquier County, Virginia, and there lived in obscurity with his daughter, Celestine Pinckney Huger, and her young children. During the war, Celly had married John W. Preston, Jr., a native South Carolinian who had served as one of her father's aides. When Jack proved to be an absentee husband, Huger bought Gordonsdale to provide a home for Celly and the children. At his farm, he raised livestock and grew orchards and crops, doing much of the labor himself. "I am entirely retired from the world," he wrote at Gordonsdale, "and only take interest in working for the benefit of my grandchildren."[4]

A change in family arrangements made it necessary for Huger to leave Gordonsdale in the autumn of 1877 and to again turn his course southward, to stay with his sister Elizabeth Pinckney Huger in Charleston.

Not until Ben's arrival did Lizzie begin to become appreciably aware of the extent to which he had been maligned. Her niece and namesake, Elizabeth Huger Prioleau (prā-lō), told her that she was excited by the observation of a man who had come to consult her husband, Dr. J. Ford Prioleau. The caller did not know the doctor or his family connection with the Hugers. Looking at a recent photograph of A. Eustis Huger, he asked who it was, and on being told, exclaimed, "Oh! The son of that General Huger who behaved so disgracefully in Virginia!" When told of the erroneous charge against the general at Seven Pines, he could only say, "I heard it in Virginia, and it was generally believed and never corrected." When Lizzie Huger asked Dr. Prioleau if her brother had been so charged, the doctor replied in the affirmative. Many believed it true, he said, in Virginia and the Carolinas. He remarked that it at first had been only an army rumor but that rumors against the general had been continued and credence given them by time. He said that McClellan's escape at White Oak Swamp had been loudly and universally pronounced Huger's failure, he having been a surgeon in Longstreet's command. When Lizzie questioned Ben concerning this statement, he replied that it had been a most unjust accusation, that he never had it in his power to destroy McClellan's army, and that Jackson, Holmes, or Magruder had quite as good a chance of doing so as he had had.[5]

Lizzie was also struck by a conversation between Ben and his "old army" friend Col. Henry J. Hunt (who had commanded McClellan's reserve artillery) one evening at the home of Cleland Huger. They were speaking of Fitz John Porter, one of Huger's best officers during the Mexican War and one of McClellan's corps commanders. Porter had been made the scapegoat by McClellan's successor and had been court-martialed out of the United States Army. Huger said that he had seen Porter, whom he had found much depressed with his situation, that he had told him to continue to seek proof for his vindication, to work steadily and perseveringly and to restore his good name for the sake of his wife, his children, and his friends, that he owed it to them. He begged Hunt to urge Porter to make every attempt to establish the truth, and if Porter died before this could be done, to finish the task for him. He had told Porter, he said, that he believed truth would prevail. Hunt echoed Huger's conviction, "Truth will prevail in the end." Lizzie noted the similarity between Porter's situation and that of her brother, whose silence in regard to his own alarmed her.[6]

Then Alfred Huger told her that he had seen Ben's name stigmatized in a northern work, *The American Cyclopaedia: A Popular Dictionary of General Knowledge.* The biographical entry ended with, "His conduct during the campaign on the peninsula was severely censured, and he was removed from active service soon after."[7] This implied official censure. Lizzie immediately informed Huger's children of the statement and asked what course should be taken to correct it. She agreed with his sons Frank Huger and Thomas Pinckney[8] that the editors should be approached at once.

On 20 November, Pinckney went to the American News Company, publishers of the encyclopedia in New York City, and addressed a personal letter to the editors. He asked for the name of the person or source of the statement and added, "I have simply to say that[,] in permitting such a statement to appear in your work[,] you have committed a great act of injustice, no doubt [unintentional] on your part, but I must make some effort to rectify it, as I cannot permit my Father[']s name to be so misrepresented . . ." He was assured that, if the statement were found to be in error, correction would be made before the issue of any subsequent copies of the volume.[9]

About a year or two before, Huger had been subjected to an attack of apoplexy; since then his health had gradually declined. Shortly before Pinckney reached the publishing company, his father suffered a violent relapse, vomiting blood intermittently for more than a day, which left him weak and nearly helpless. His voice became very low and his speech thick. Almost inarticulate, he complained of pain all over his body and slept most of the time. The doctor came twice a day but could only watch over him. All agreed that he should not be disturbed by the present issue.

For several days, Huger's health seemed to have improved slightly. Sometimes he enjoyed seeing people and talking with old friends. On the twenty-eighth, however, he began calling for his children. Lizzie had wanted him to write a denial to the published assertion but realized that it was now too late. Believing her brother near death, she questioned him concerning the censure ascribed by the encyclopedia. Then she began writing a memoir:

> *Genl B Huger*
> *I could not venture to tell him of the report of his*
> *name in the American Encyclopedia. [H]e was too ill*
> *to be disturbed by such scandal—but his mind still*
> *clear, particularly on past events. I asked him if he*
> *had never been "censured" for his military conduct.*
> *[H]e said "never by any court, or his superiors[;] there*
> *was that 'report' of Longstreet[']s—but he had*
> *retracted it, & made all the excuse in his power. Genl*
> *Joseph Johnston had never said any thing [in his*
> Narrative of Military Operations Directed During the
> Late War Between the States *(1874)] which he thought*
> *he ought to have done—said he had searched his book*
> *but he had not mentioned him [in a retraction]." I*
> *asked how long after that report was made, was it*
> *that he was informed it was desirable [that] he should*

give up his command. [H]e said a month, or more,
several weeks he believed—said he had told Randolph,
then Sec^y of War [that] he would resign if they wanted
him to do so, but Mr Randolph begged him not, said
such men as you we want &c—said "Genl Lee spoke
to me about giving up the command[,] said he was
sure I must be glad to avoid such scenes of carnage
farther, he would gladly do so, & I could serve the
Confederacy in another way,['] &c. I never could
venture to ask him more, so failed to ask his signature
to the above that he had not been "censured" by com-
petent authority. I once heard him desire an officer to
urge a man similarly situated to make every effort to
establish the truth—for his children & friends—& ever
if he died—to clear his good name—

I wish the same done for [my brother].
EP Huger[10]

1st Dec^r

Six days after the interview, on 7 December 1877, Huger
died. Frank wired the news to Celly, who, unwell herself, had
been unable to make the trip to Charleston from her home in
Columbia. On the eighth, she penned: "I received yesterday
your telegram. It seems as if one year had passed since then.
While not being there to see that precious face once more is
almost more than I can bear—namely—that I will never see it
again. . . . I am trying so hard to bear up as he would wish me. I
know my grief is very selfish[,] for he has wished so much to
go[,] but I feel as if almost all had gone with him. . . . God in
His mercy be with you and give you strength to bear this grief
is the earnest prayer of your devoted sister."[11] A close neigh-
bor near Gordonsdale, Mrs. Corrie G. Peyton, whom Huger had
affectionately called "Daughter," wrote to Celly that her
father had been "a true friend to me, more like a near relative,
and will always be held up to my boys, especially his godson,
as the very embodiment of purity, courage, honor, and good-
ness."[12] Meta D. Huger, a niece of the general, wrote to her:

I had not heard until your letter of your sorrow but I
feared [that death] was coming. I do not know why I say

"feared" because I do believe if any man is ripe for heaven[,] he was & why should I or you[,] his well-loved child, wish to stretch him longer on the back of this rough world? God has taken him but not before he was ready & willing to depart & be with Christ[,] which is far better.[13] Only the world is growing very empty for us who are left behind. He was the last of those men of our name who have made it historic . . . The women know how to value them, what we do not know is where to look for their peers among the living.[14]

10. *Aftermath*

In accordance with his own wish, Huger's remains were taken by train to Baltimore. The body arrived at Union Depot (later Pennsylvania Station) on the afternoon of 11 December, was taken to Green Mount Cemetery, and laid by the side of his wife and son in the presence of relatives and friends.

On the day of the funeral, the Baltimore *Gazette* reported: "The death of General Benjamin Huger has revived a controversy concerning his transfer to the trans-Mississippi department just after the close of the battles around Richmond. Owing to some conflict of authority or confusion of orders[,] Generals Huger and Magruder failed to perform the work expected of them at and about Malvern Hill. Public opinion at the time visited the failure upon General Huger."[1] Concerning this, Celly wrote to Frank: "my heart goes down to my boots—I should a thousand times[—]and I feel sure he would too[—] have his name forgotten by the world than have one of those dreadful newspaper controversies that the Confederates are so fond of. In mercy don't have those ugly sores that killed Mother and made Father an old and broken[-]spirited man opened again."[2]

While Celly was opposed to public controversy, she agreed that the statement in the encyclopedia should be corrected. The writer of the statement having cited as his authority the official reports of Lee, Johnston, Longstreet, and others, Pinckney proposed applying to Davis for an opposing statement. Lizzie suggested that a biographical vindication be written for the historical societies of South Carolina and Virginia. While she would write of Ben's early years, Frank would prepare his father's vindication, providing evidence from statements by Davis, McClellan, R. H. Anderson, and others, including perhaps Johnston and Longstreet, and by the memoir Lizzie had written after interviewing Huger on 1 December. The general biographical portion was begun at once.

Initiating his investigation, Frank requested Davis to write a statement of the reasons which led to Huger's removal from the command of his division, "which we had understood was not predicated on official censure or for any want of confidence in his zeal for & earnestness in the cause," adding, "I am well aware & shall never live long enough to forget the gross injustice with which news-paper scriblers & petty politicians who couldn't use him abused him, as I shall not [forget] the [courageous] forbearance & dignity with which he suffered it."[3] Frank's letter was answered:

Miss City   14th Jany 1878

My Dear Sir,

Yours of the 5th inst. has been received. You should have felt no reluctance in calling upon me, as the high regard & esteem in which I always held your Father might have assured you of my sympathy with you in the matter on which you address me. I have not a copy of the work to which you refer and your letter gives me the first information of the reflection it contains upon the late Genl Huger. I cannot recall the time or the manner of your Father's retirement from the command of a division in the field and can give you only my recollection of preceeding [sic] events.

Genl Huger commanded the post & district of Norfolk and by a stubborn maintenance of his position even after the retreat of the forces from Yorktown, secured to the Confederacy, the valuable material & machinery, which was removed from the Navy Yard at Norfolk to Richmond[,] and then withdrew his command in good order.

For this, I then & have often since, expressed my high commendation. At the Battle of Seven Pines, he was ordered to move by a certain road, & found a stream which he had to cross, swollen & the bridge destroyed, so that he could not pass his artillery over it on that route. The time employed in repairing the bridge was subsequently complained of by Genl Longstreet & became the subject of a controversy on which you can no doubt get more accurate information than I am able to give you. In the pursuit of McClellan's retreating army, Genl Huger's Division was on the extreme left, & the time occupied in the passage of the White Oak Swamp was regarded by Genl Lee as greater than was needful & proper. Of the merits of the case[,] I did not consider myself then competent to judge & am certainly less so now than then for I have forgotten much & learned nothing in regard to the matter.

This much I can unreservedly say. I never doubted the zeal & fidelity of Genl Huger to the cause to which he had sacrificed the associations & the ambitions of his early life; and it is not possible that any action of mine ever implied any such doubt of him.

Like yourself[,] I regret the criminations & recriminations which have resulted from the discussion of the events of the war.

The Army of the Confederate States achieved enough to give to all its parts a distributive share of military glory sufficient to satisfy any reasonable demand. It might have been left to their numerous enemies to disparage those to whom fortune had shown the least favour.

Yours faithfully,
Jefferson Davis[4]

Col. Frank Huger

The failure of Davis's memory—even had he known the facts—rendered his statement worthless in opposition to that of the encyclopedia. Celly's husband then applied to the ex-president and was answered:

Miss City P.O. 18th Jan 1878.

Col John W Preston
  My Dear Sir
    *A few days before the receipt of your letter, one
from your brother-in-law Frank Huger, making similar
inquiries to yours[,] was received & answered. I in
vain endeavored then & since to recall the time and
circumstances under which Genl Huger was relieved
from the command of a Division. I well remember the
high appreciation in which I held his services as a
commanding officer at Norfolk and the permanent
benefit resulting to the Confederacy from his conduct
on that occasion. As well from my personal as professional esteem for Genl Huger[,] I cannot believe that
any order reflecting [adversely] upon him as to his
patriotism, zeal and fidelity could ever have received
my approval. I remember that at the Battle of Seven
Pines, questions arose between him & Genl Longstreet,
& that the latter as I thought, unjustly, attributed to
Genl Huger delay in the execution of his orders.
Subsequently, in the pursuit of McClellan's retreating
army, I remember that Genl Lee thought that Genl
Huger was too slow in his movements and that we (I
being on the field with him at Frazier's Farm) were
disappointed at the non-arrival of Genl Huger's
Division. Whether Genl Lee took any official action in
the matter I cannot say—if so, it must appear among
the archives at the War Department, now said to be in
Washington city. Perhaps one of the members [of
Congress] from S. Carolina would feel sufficient
interest for a name so honored in Carolina's history as
to seek & attain the requisite information. Please
present my affectionate remembrance to Mrs Preston.
Mrs Davis is in Memphis, if here would certainly join
me in this.*

Truly your friend,
Jefferson Davis[5]

Reflecting on this statement—of no more value than the first—Lizzie wrote: "How I wish I had know[n] of all this when twice with Gen Lee. I feel sure I could have got his testimony. I knew *how* he had failed to be the friend he had seemed . . . but he had outlived that & spoke to me (who was shy of him at first) of my good Brother in [the] highest terms—he felt *down* himself then & was[,] I believe [,] ready to do justice—but that time has *gone*;[6] dont let any more escape you & Pinck, my dear Frank." "Continue always to collect all the means, get all the records & information you can, & continue to prepare" for the biographical vindication.[7]

After reading the two statements from Davis, Pinckney wrote to Frank: "It is of no use for you to write to Johnston or Longstreet. It would be entirely humiliating to you and they would not give you any satisfaction. I care very little myself what these Yankee people [the encyclopedists] say, and I know how much detraction was put so unjustly & falsely on him by those who should have been his friends. . . . I know Father was always so opposed to any newspaper controversy that I should not like to enter into one, and it would just lead to very little results."[8]

Confronted by the impossible task of vindicating his father, Frank wrote to Lizzie expressing his utter despair. Lizzie replied: "there is[,] you say[,] no hurry to spread the truth & few care to read History. Still it must be written, & read by some[,] for 'truth will in the end prevail'!"[9]

Appendix: Maps

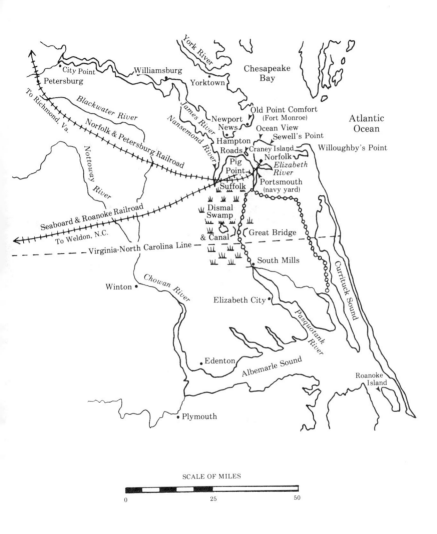

The Department of Norfolk and its vicinity

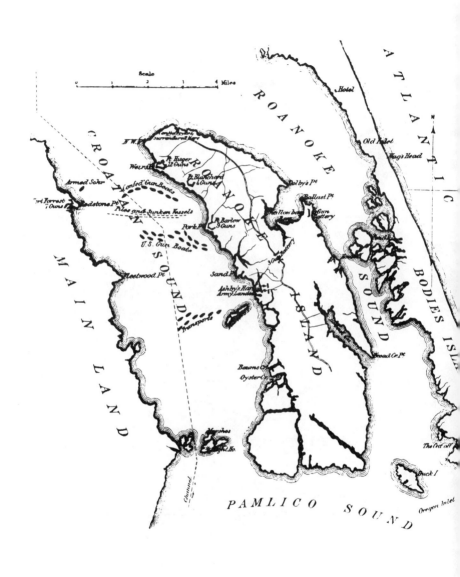

Map of the Battle of Roanoke Island.
Kean Archives, Philadelphia, Pennsylvania.

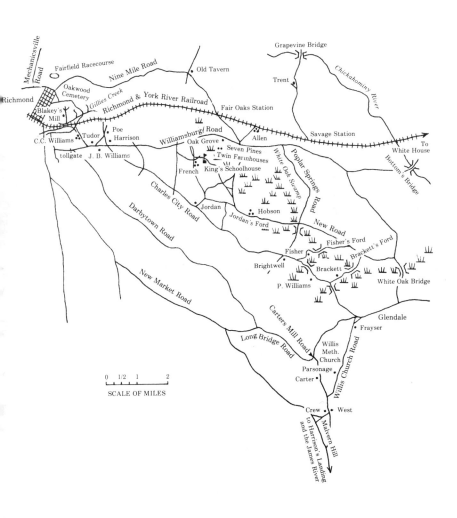

Richmond to Malvern Hill

132

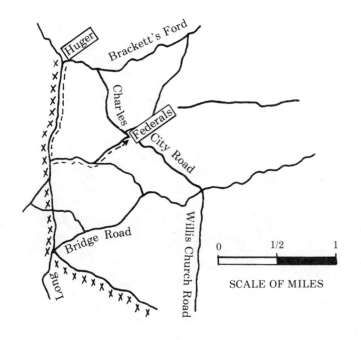

XXX Armistead-Wright Line of March
——— Line of March as Huger Intended

Armistead's Misunderstanding
(Morning of 1 July 1862)

Notes

Works and collections cited frequently in the notes are identified by the following abbreviations:

B & L	*Battles and Leaders of the Civil War: Being for the Most Part Contributions by Union and Confederate Officers.* 4 vols. Edited by Robert U. Johnson and Clarence C. Buel. New York: Thomas Yoseloff, Inc., 1956.
FC	The Frost Collection of Benjamin Huger Papers
Lee's Dispatches	*Lee's Dispatches: Unpublished Letters of General Robert E. Lee, C.S.A., to Jefferson Davis and the War Department of the Confederate States of America, 1862-65.* Edited by Douglas S. Freeman. New York: G. P. Putnam's Sons, 1957.
ORA	*The War of the Rebellion: A Compilation of the Official Records of the Union and Confederate Armies.* 70 vols. in 127 and index. Washington, D.C.: U.S. Government Printing Office, 1880-1901.
ORN	*Official Records of the Union and Confederate Navies in the War of the Rebellion.* 30 vols. and index. Washington, D.C.: U.S. Government Printing Office, 1894-1927.

RC   The Rutherfoord Collection of Benjamin
                            Huger Papers

WDR   War Department Records (National Archives)

References not listed in the selective bibliography are given in full in
the notes. When full references are found in the bibliography, the
notes reference includes only the last name of the author and page
number(s).

Chapter 1. *Introduction*

1. Huger to Lizzie Huger, Dublin, 2 July 1828, *RC*.

2. U.S. Congress Senate. *Message from the President*, p. 380.

3. In time of war, a brevet was awarded for gallantry or meritorious
conduct or both. As an honorary promotion, brevet rank was not accompanied by the authority or emoluments of real rank; the brevetted
officer was merely addressed by his (highest) brevet. However, when
a brevetted officer served on courts-martial or held a position above
that for which his regular army rank was designated, he was entitled
by law to the precedence and pay of his brevet and to display on his
uniform the insignias of that advanced rank. At any event, the action
for which a brevet was awarded was considered a highlight of a
soldier's career.

4. George W. Cullum, *Biographical Register of the Officers and
Graduates of the U.S. Military Academy at West Point, N.Y., from Its
Establishment in 1802 . . .* , 3d ed., 3 vols. (New York: Houghton,
Mifflin and Co., 1891), 1, p. 344.

Chapter 2. *"God Help Us"*

1. Huger to father, Paris, 29 July 1828, *RC*.

2. Col. Francis K. Huger was a Unionist and directed his efforts to
forestall secession. It is interesting to note that, in spite of their differing political views, Colonel Huger and the Hon. John C. Calhoun
remained close friends, met often, and dined at each other's houses
frequently. Ben's sister Lizzie remembered, "My Father differed in
politics from the reigning party, yet it made no difference in social
intercourse. Mr. Calhoun was a nullifier, my Father and friends of his
name were not, and when parties [spirits] ran high, many would have
dropped a man they could not move, but my Father continued good
friends to the end with all" (Mary Esther Huger, *The Recollection of a
Happy Childhood*, p. 15).

3. Lafayette to Huger, La Grange, 1 November 1828, in the estate of
Huger's late granddaughter Mrs. Julia Monniche of Austin, Texas.

Lafayette wrote the letter in English.

4. Kinsay Johns to Huger, Saint Louis, 8 December 1860, *RC*.

5. *ORA*, ser. I, vol. 1, p. 79.

6. Abner Doubleday, *Reminiscences of Forts Sumter and Moultrie in 1860-'61* (New York: Harper & Brothers, Publishers, 1876), p. 42.

7. *ORA*, ser. I, vol. 1, pp. 83–84; Cleland Huger to Huger, Charleston, 14 December 1860, *RC*.

8. Ibid., pp. 84–85.

9. Ibid., pp. 87–88.

10. Cleland Huger to Huger in note 7.

11. Draft of Huger to Scott [Washington] 12 December 1860, and Huger's endorsement thereon, *RC*.

12. *ORA*, ser. I, vol. 1, pp. 95–98, 100–101; "Documents: Narrative and Letter of William Henry Trescot, Concerning the Negotiations Between South Carolina and President Buchanan in December, 1860," *The American Historical Review*, 89 vols. to date (New York: The Macmillan Co., 1908), 13, p. 539.

13. Cleland Huger to Huger, Charleston, 24 December 1860 (telegram), *RC*.

14. Copy of Alfred Huger to Huger, Charleston, 25 December 1860, *RC*, later delivered to Huger by Alfred Ravenel; Alfred Huger to Pickens, Charleston, 27 December 1860, Item 15, Reel No. 1, Francis W. Pickens Papers, Manuscript Division, Library of Congress.

15. From the outline draft of Huger to Alfred Huger (n.p., n.d.) entitled "Why I cannot," *RC*.

16. Copy of Alfred Huger to Huger in note 14. Excess punctuation is omitted.

17. Mary Chesnut, *The Private Mary Chesnut: The Unpublished Civil War Diaries*, edited by C. Van Woodward and Elisabeth Muhlenfeld (New York: Oxford University Press, 1984), p. 78.

18. Alfred Huger to Huger, Charleston, 27 December 1860 (telegram); Gourdin to Huger, Charleston, 28 December 1860 (telegram); Ravenel to Huger, Charleston, 28 December 1860, *RC*.

19. Ravenel to Huger, Charleston, 29 December 1860 (telegram); Cleland Huger to Huger, Charleston, 30 December 1860 (telegram), *RC*. In expectation of Huger's arrival, a reorganization of the state forces was published in the *Charleston Daily Courier* on the twenty-ninth, the commander to rank as major general.

20. Trescot to Huger, Washington, 31 December 1860 (telegram), *RC*.

21. As commander in chief of the Army of South Carolina, Huger would be the only major general of the state. The policy of the Confed-

erate president in appointing officers from the United States Army
was to advance no one more than one grade in rank. Since the rank of
lieutenant general was not used early in the war (with the exception of
Scott), Huger would be promoted into the Confederate States Army
as a full general.

22. Ravenel to Huger, Charleston, 4 January 1861 (telegram), *RC*.

23. Draft of Huger to Alfred Huger, Baltimore, 3 January 1861, *RC*.
Excess punctuation is omitted.

24. *ORA*, ser. I, vol. 14, p. 515.

25. Doubleday, *Reminiscences*, p. 114; Cleland Huger to Huger in
note 13, for which see p. 17.

26. Draft of Huger to Alfred Huger, Washington, 15 January 1861,
RC. Excess punctuation is omitted.

27. Alfred Huger to Huger [Charleston] 17 January 1861, *RC*; *ORA*,
ser. I, vol. 1, pp. 143–46; Doubleday, *Reminiscences*, pp. 113–14.

28. Bragg to Huger, New Orleans, 10 February 1861; Hagner to
Huger, Saint Louis Arsenal, 11 February 1861, *RC*.

29. Beauregard's position in South Carolina was merely temporary.
After Huger declined the position, no permanent commander of the
army was named.

30. Frame 0511, Roll 27, Microcopy 619, Record Group 94, Letters
Received by the Office of the Adjutant General, *WDR*.

31. See note 30, frame 0509.

Chapter 3. *An Exile in Virginia*

1. Memoir of Lizzie Huger, Charleston [January 1878] *RC*.

2. Personal file of Benjamin Huger, *WDR*; Lizzie Huger to Frank
Huger, Charleston, 6 May 1878, *RC*.

3. Letcher to Huger, Richmond, 22 May 1861, *FC*; Lee to Huger
[Richmond] 23 May 1861, *RC*; *ORA*, ser. I, vol. 2, p. 867; Ibid., vol. 51,
pt. 2, pp. 102, 106, 347; *Calendar of Virginia State Papers and Other
Manuscripts from January 1, 1836, to April 15, 1869; Preserved in the
Capitol at Richmond*, edited by H. W. Flournoy (New York: Kraus
Reprint Corp., 1968), p. 135.

4. See Douglas S. Freeman, *R. E. Lee: A Biography*, 4 vols. (New
York: Charles Scribner's Sons, 1934), 1, pp. 579–94.

5. *ORA*, ser. I, vol. 9, p. 114.

6. Ibid., p.133.

7. Ibid., pp. 110, 113, 115.

8. Marshall, pp. 16–17; *ORA*, ser. I, vol. 9, p.110.

9. *ORN*, ser. I, vol. 6, p. 599; *ORA*, ser. I, vol. 9, pp. 81–83, 181.

10. Davis to Huger, Richmond, 27 February 1862 (telegram), *RC*, reproduced in *ORA*, ser. I, vol. 9, p. 45.

11. *ORA*, ser. I, vol. 9, p. 55.

12. Davis to Huger, Richmond, 26 February 1862 (private letter), *RC*, reproduced in *ORA*, ser. I, vol. 9, p. 45.

13. Huger to Tattnall, Richmond, 2 September 1862, Benjamin Huger Papers, Duke University Library, quoted *in extenso*, p. 112; *ORN*, ser. II, vol. 1, p. 634.

14. *ORN*, ser. II, vol. 1, p. 635; copy (ca. August 1862) of Huger to Lee, Hq. Dept. of Norfolk, 3 May 1862, *RC*.

15. Huger, "*Notes*, made at the request of Genl BC Howard to McCabe's life of Genl Lee, pgs. 154–155[,] 156–157," Baltimore, June 1867, *RC*.

Chapter 4. *Seven Pines: A Military Nightmare*

1. Huger to Cleland Huger, near Drewry's Bluff, 28 July 1862, *RC*.

2. *ORA*, ser. I, vol. 11, pt. 1, p. 938.

3. Ibid.

4. The headings of papers written by members of Huger's staff, in conjunction with contemporary maps, reveal that Huger's headquarters were established at J. B. Williams's farmhouse. According to Huger (to John Huger, Baltimore, 20 June 1867, Doc. 7, Edward Porter Alexander Papers, Southern Historical Collection, University of North Carolina Library), Hill's headquarters were half a mile from his. Harrison's farmhouse was the only establishment at or reasonably near the specified distance. Lieutenant Sloan's letter to General Smith *(B & L* [1887] 1956, 2, p. 228) confirms the location of Hill's headquarters. The plain mentioned by Sloan was part of Williams's farm, which was used as Huger's artillery camp.

5. Huger to John Huger in note 4; *B&L* [1887] 1956, 2, p. 228.

6. Memoir of Rev. G. W. Finley, D.D., 17 March 1897, Box No. 13, Jedediah Hotchkiss Papers, Manuscript Division, Library of Congress; Huger to John Huger in note 4; Huger, "A Card," *Richmond Examiner*, 25 August 1862, p. 1, col. 3, New York State Library at Albany.

7. Samuel E. Mays, "Famous Battles as a Confederate Private Saw Them," *Tyler's Quarterly Historical and Genealogical Magazine*, 33 vols., edited by Lyon G. Tyler (New York: Kraus Reprint Corp., 1967), 4, pp. 391, 392.

8. Douglas S. Freeman, *Lee's Lieutenants: A Study in Command*, 3 vols. (New York: Charles Scribner's Sons, 1942), 1, pp. 164-65.

9. James Longstreet, *From Manassas to Appomattox: Memoirs of the Civil War in America*, edited by James I. Robertson, Jr. (Bloomington: Indiana University Press, 1960), p. 103.

10. The conclusion is drawn from the new evidence presented in this and subsequent chapters.

11. *B&L* [1887] 1956, 2, p. 212.

12. Ibid., p. 229.

13. *ORA*, ser. I, vol. 11, pt. 1, p. 942.

14. Huger, "*Notes*, made at the request of Genl BC Howard to McCabe's life of Genl Lee, Pgs. 98-99, 103," Baltimore, June 1867, Doc. 7, Edward Porter Alexander Papers, Southern Historical Collection, University of North Carolina Library.

15. Longstreet's premise that an officer could gain or lose seniority in the transition from United States to Confederate States service is valid. For example, Johnston lost seniority to three former juniors, Lee among them. However, sufficient evidence that Longstreet possessed full knowledge of Huger's seniority is provided by the fact that he included Huger in his scheme to rid the army of his seniors and by the detail of his statement to Huger claiming seniority. Huger was aware that Longstreet had lied to him when he wrote, "I also had the misfortune to be the Senior Maj^r Genl and many juniors would like me out of *their* way" (see chapter 4, note 1). Also, Smith seemed to be aware that Longstreet knew Huger ranked him (see Frank Huger to father, Ruther Glen (Virginia), 24 April 1863, p. 114).

16. Freeman, *Lee's Lieutenants* (see chapter 4, note 8), 1, p. 259.

17. Finley memoir and *Richmond Examiner* in chapter 4, note 6; *B&L* [1887] 1956, 2, p. 229; *ORA*, ser. I, vol. 11, pt. 1, pp. 938, 940, 986; *ORA*, ser. I, vol. 11, pt. 3, pp. 563, 564.

18. *Battle-fields of the South*, p. 238. In a postwar letter to a former Union officer, Longstreet stated positively (G. W. Smith, p. 152) that Johnston's plan was to turn the Union left at daylight by Huger's division moving across the head of White Oak Swamp on a passable route for infantry to the Federal left and rear, Huger's attack to be followed by Hill's, the latter to be supported if need be by Longstreet's division, and Whiting's attack to be in accordance with Hill's movements. The plan failed, Longstreet stated, because Huger did not reach the field. (Note the relationship between this account of the plan and Davis's incorrect defense of Huger in Davis, 2, pp. 125-27; see also Davis's postwar letters in regard to the subject, pp. 124, 125.)

19. *Battle-fields of the South*, p. 242.

20. Huger to John Huger in chapter 4, note 4.

21. *ORA*, ser. I, vol. 11, pt. 3, p. 570.

22. Ibid.

23. *ORA*, ser. I, vol. 11, pt. 2, p. 787.

24. *ORA*, ser. I, vol. 11, pt. 3, p. 580.

25. *ORA*, ser. I, vol. 11, pt. 1, p. 940.

26. Ibid., p. 941.

27. Ibid., pp. 933, 934, 935.

28. *ORA*, ser. I, vol. 11, pt. 3, p. 571; *Richmond Examiner* in chapter 4, note 6; see p. 119.

Chapter 5. *King's Schoolhouse: On the Defensive*

1. Brent, p. 205; Longstreet, *From Manassas to Appomattox*, pp. 142, 158; *Lee's Dispatches*, p. 11; *ORA*, ser. I, vol. 11, pt. 2, p. 550; Jubal Early, *Lieutenant General Jubal Anderson Early, C.S.A.: Autobiographical Sketch and Narrative of the War Between the States*, edited by R. H. Early (Philadelphia: J. B. Lippincott Co., 1912), p. 89; G. Moxley Sorrel, *Recollections of a Confederate Staff Officer*, edited by Bell I. Wiley (Jackson, Tenn.: McCowat-Mercer Press, Inc., 1958), p. 69.

2. *ORA*, ser. I, vol. 14, p. 524.

3. *Lee's Dispatches*, pp. 10–11, 14; *ORA*, ser. I, vol. 14, pp. 569, 572.

Chapter 7. *White Oak Swamp: The Pursuit Blunders*

1. *ORA*, ser. I, vol. 11, pt. 2, pp. 98, 788.

2. Brent, p. 181.

3. *ORA*, ser. I, vol. 11, pt. 2, p. 789.

4. *ORA*, ser. I, vol. 11, pt. 2, pp. 664, 665, 675, 680, 681.

5. R. Taylor, p. 103.

6. Writing some four years after the event, Jackson's chief of staff stated that the Stonewall Brigade had accompanied the general to Magruder's position (Dabney, p. 459); but he was mistaken (*ORA*, ser. I, vol. 11, pt. 2, pp. 571, 589, 627).

7. *ORA*, ser. I, vol. 11, pt. 2, pp. 663, 665, 681, 687, 726.

8. Finley memoir in chapter 4, note 6.

9. Ibid.

10. John B. Jones, *A Rebel War Clerk's Diary*, 2 vols., edited by Earl S. Miers (New York: Sagamore Press, 1958), 1, p. 140; Huger to Cleland Huger in chapter 4, note 1. The divisional strength given by Huger apparently excludes Wright's brigade, which was detached during the battle.

11. *Battle-fields of the South*, p. 356.

12. Davis, 2, pp. 142–43, 144; R. Taylor, p. 99; *ORA*, ser. I, vol. 11, pt. 2, pp. 518, 532, 906–7.

13. *ORA*, ser. I, vol. 11, pt. 2, p. 908.

14. Longstreet, *From Manassas to Appomattox*, p. 139.

15. *ORA*, ser. I, vol. 11, pt. 2, p. 718.

16. Brent, pp. 193–94.

17. *ORA*, ser. I, vol. 11, pt. 2, p. 435.

18. *B&L* [1887] 1956, 2, p. 378.

19. *ORA*, ser. I, vol. 11, pt. 2, pp. 810–11.

20. Huger to Cleland Huger in chapter 4, note 1. In this letter to his brother, Huger pointed out, "The fact was McClelland [sic] had the time on me, and the track and got ahead, and blocked the way both on Genl Jackson & myself near White oak bridge." Huger's sister Lizzie wrote, "Cleland says yr Father *proved* that waters they [Huger and Jackson] were unable to cross, prevented his being up to time" (Lizzie Huger to Frank Huger in chapter 3, note 2).

21. Capt. Thomas J. Goree to mother, near Richmond, 21 July 1862, in the care of Mr. Henri Gerard Noordberg of Huntsville, Texas. The writer was a member of Longstreet's staff.

Chapter 7. *Malvern Hill: The Enemy Escapes*

1. John Goode, *Recollections of a Lifetime* (New York: Neale Publishing Co., 1906), p. 58.

2. *B&L* [1887] 1956, 2, p. 391.

3. Ibid., p. 388.

4. *ORA*, ser. I, vol. 11, pt. 2, p. 677.

5. See chapter 6, note 21.

6. Finley memoir in chapter 4, note 6.

7. *ORA*, ser. I, vol. 11, pt. 2, p. 669. Due to the rough terrain, the lack of knowledge of it, and the occasional difficulty in locating commanders in the field, the delivery of orders was sometimes delayed for several hours.

8. *ORA*, ser. I, vol. 11, pt. 2, pp. 677–78.

9. Finley memoir in chapter 4, note 6.

10. Brent, p. 212.

11. Lee's order to Huger (*ORA*, ser. I, vol. 11, pt. 2, p. 686) was not written until after Magruder called for reinforcements. If Huger had received an order to the same effect earlier than the aforementioned, he failed to mention it either to Brent (Brent, p. 213) or later in his official report of the Seven Days (*ORA*, ser. I, vol. 11, pt. 2, p. 790).

12. *ORA*, ser. I, vol. 11, pt. 2, p. 686.

13. Ibid.

14. J. Watts De Peyster, "A Military Memoir of William Mahone, Major-General in the Confederate Army," *The Historical Magazine* . . ., 23 vols. (Morrisania, N.Y.: Henry B. Dawson, 1870), ser. II, vol. 7, p. 395.

15. *ORA*, ser. I, vol. 11, pt. 2, pp. 678, 790.

16. Brent, p. 233.

17. Freeman, *R. E. Lee*, 2, p. 218.

18. *ORA*, ser. I, vol. 11, pt. 2, p. 619.

19. Huger to John Huger in chapter 4, note 4.

Chapter 8. *The Banishment*

1. Johnston, trained and experienced as a topographical engineer, also had been negligent before and during his withdrawal from Yorktown. Roads in that jungle of dense woodlands and swamps were often as confusing as they possibly could be. Spellings of the names of some of them were inconsistent with their phonetic pronunciations. Some changed names beyond an inconspicuous intersection. Unusually frequent were two entirely different roads bearing the same name. Others had two or three different names. Still others had no names at all. (In the case of roads with more than one name, the most popular name is used in the text and on the map "Richmond to Malvern Hill.")

For details on the subject of maps and guides, see *B&L*, 2, pp. 352, 355, 361, 395, 431; Brent, pp. 206, 207; Dabney, p. 457; Davis, 2, pp. 142-43, 144; Henderson, pp. 21, 25, 26n., 36, 57, 72, 86, 88; Longstreet, pp. 139, 142, 143; R. Taylor, pp. 98-102, 104, 105, 107; W. Taylor, pp. 73, 74; *ORA*, ser. I, vol. 11, pt. 1, pp. 152-53; ibid., pt. 2, pp. 496, 497, 520, 522, 537, 568, 570, 668, 675-77, 718, 776; *ORA*, ser. I, vol. 47, pt. 2, p. 1306; Otto Eisenschiml, *The Hidden Face of the Civil War* (New York: Bobbs-Merrill, 1961), pp. 217-22; William C. Oates, *The War Between the Union and the Confederacy and Its Lost Opportunities* . . . (New York: The Neale Publishing Co., 1905), pp. 123, 126-27; Robert Stiles, *Four Years Under Marse Robert* (New

York: The Neale Publishing Co., 1903), pp. 106–7.

2. See chapter 6, note 21.

3. See chapter 6, note 21.

4. Lizzie Huger to Frank Huger in chapter 3, note 2.

5. Before Seven Pines, it will be recalled, Lee had insisted to Governor Pickens that Huger could not be spared from the army defending Richmond; after the battle, he reversed his decision.

6. Alexander, p. 151.

7. Huger to Cleland Huger in chapter 4, note 1.

8. See *Southern Historical Society Papers*, 52 vols. (Richmond: The William Byrd Press, Inc., 1925), 45, pp. 192–97.

9. *ORA*, ser. I, vol. 11, pt. 3, p. 643.

10. A court of inquiry is similar to a civil grand jury, whereas a court-martial bears a similar relationship to a court of criminal jurisdiction. The former gathers available evidence and determines if a court-martial is warranted.

11. See chapter 3, note 13. Excess punctuation is omitted.

12. *ORA*, ser. I, vol. 11, pt. 1, p. 939.

13. Huger to president, Richmond, 14 October 1862, in the possession of the author.

14. Draft of Huger to secretary of war, n.p. [November 1862] *RC*.

15. G. W. Smith had begun gathering evidence from key witnesses on Longstreet's conduct at Seven Pines.

16. Typescript copy of Frank Huger to father, Ruther Glen (Virginia), 24 April 1863, *RC*.

17. Huger to Frank Huger, Columbia, 30 April 1863, *RC*.

18. Huger to wife, Marshall, 6 April 1864, *RC*.

Chapter 9. *The Final Ruin*

1. See chapter 4, note 14.

2. See chapter 3, note 15.

3. Huger's 1867 diary, *RC*.

4. Huger to Colston, The Plains (Virginia), 3 July 1872, Doc. 2574, Raleigh E. Colston Papers, Southern Historical Collection, University of North Carolina Library.

5. Lizzie Huger to Frank Huger in chapter 3, note 2.

6. Lizzie Huger to Frank Huger in chapter 3, note 2. Porter was later

exonerated officially. See Otto Eisenschiml, *The Celebrated Case of Fitz John Porter: An American Dreyfus Affair* (Indianapolis: Bobbs-Merrill, 1950).

7. *The American Cyclopaedia: A Popular Dictionary of General Knowledge*, 16 vols., edited by George Ripley and Charles A. Dana (New York: D. Appleton and Co., 1874), 9, p. 32.

8. In order to receive an inheritance from his maternal grandfather, Col. Thomas Pinckney, Jr., who wanted his name to be carried on by one of his descendants, Thomas Pinckney Huger, as a young child, was required to legally omit his surname. Colonel Pinckney died while the name was in the process of being changed, and the wealth was inherited by Pinckney's cousin Thomas Pinckney. (Mrs. Julia Huger Monniche, interview with the author, Austin, Texas, May 1971.)

9. Pinckney to Ripley and Dana, New York, 20 November 1877; Pinckney to Frank Huger, New York, 20 November 1877; Milner to Pinckney, New York, 23 November 1877, *RC*.

10. From *RC*. Excess punctuation is omitted.

11. Celly Preston to Frank Huger [Columbia] 8 December 1877; *RC*.

12. Peyton to Celly Preston, n.p., n.d., *RC*.

13. See Philippians 1:23.

14. Meta Huger to Celly Preston, Baltimore, 10 December 1877, *RC*.

Chapter 10. *Aftermath*

1. *Baltimore Gazette*, 11 December 1877, p. 2, col. 3, Library of Congress.

2. Celly Preston to Frank Huger [Columbia] 5 January 1878, *RC*.

3. Draft of Frank Huger to Davis [Lynchburg] January 1878, *RC*. The letter is printed in *Jefferson Davis, Constitutionalist: His Letters, Papers, and Speeches*, 10 vols., edited by Dunbar Rowland (Jackson: Printed for the Mississippi Department of Archives and History, 1923), 8, pp. 66–67.

4. From *RC*.

5. From *RC*.

6. Lee had died in 1870.

7. Lizzie Huger to Frank Huger in chapter 3, note 2.

8. Pinckney to Frank Huger, New York, 30 January 1878, *RC*.

9. Lizzie Huger to Frank Huger in chapter 3, note 2.

Selective Critical Bibliography

My intention was to obtain substantially all the extant information relating to Huger, and no effort was spared to reach this end. Many hundreds of books, manuscripts, pamphlets, magazines, newspapers, letters, telegrams, and other documents were studied from the Library of Congress, a number of state, university, and local libraries, the National Archives, the West Point Archives, more than ten state archives and their respective historical societies, the Office of Military History of the Department of the Army, numerous museums, and private collections of documents.

By far the most significant sources of information used in the preparation of the text are family collections of documents. Undeniably a sentimentalist, Huger saved most if not all of his papers. Even receipts for clothing he had purchased while touring Europe in the late 1820s could be found among his accumulation after his death. At that time, the papers were divided among members of the family and later passed from one generation to the next.

The Rutherfoord Collection of Huger's papers (now available as the Benjamin Huger Papers microfilm M-2277-2279, Manuscripts Department, University of Virginia Library), and the largest such collection, is in the

estate of the late Mrs. Aurelia Huger Rutherfoord of Charlottesville, Virginia, a daughter of Colonel Frank Huger, C.S.A., and
granddaughter of General Huger. The collection includes
diaries, private and official letters, telegrams, military papers,
miscellaneous documents, a small library of related books,
daguerreotypes, and photographs.

In the estate of the late Mrs. Julia Huger Monniche of
Austin, Texas, a sister of Mrs. Rutherfoord, are a few photographs and letters, a miniature of Huger (reproduced as a plate
in this book), his 1828 diary describing his first European tour,
and his Sword of Honor.

The Frost Collection of Huger's papers (the Benjamin
Huger Papers microfilm M-2279, Manuscripts Department,
University of Virginia Library), formerly owned by the late
Mr. John Preston Frost of Charleston, South Carolina, a great-
grandson of the general, consists primarily of private letters
written during the early Mexican War and late Civil War
periods. Photographs and portraits are also a part of this
collection.

Owing to their wide diversity in so many subjects, not
all the documents have been used (nor have all the documents
used been cited in notes); nevertheless, their value solicits the
attention of the serious student and scholar. One obvious
hazard of brevity is oversimplification, yet detailed inventories
of these collections would add voluminous length to this
summation.

Of particular importance with regard to the general's
official correspondence are the War Department Records of
the Old Military Records Section of the National Archives.
This prodigious collection includes his personal file and communications received and sent during his forty years of service
in the United States and Confederate States Armies.

In the course of my study, I have carefully consulted
every available book mentioning the general. Only works of
special assistance are appended in this bibliography. For
others used on occasion, the reader may refer to those cited in
notes. For locating the most important periodicals, the reader
is invited to follow the same procedure, which avoids a
repellent list of references. Those titles appearing in quotation
marks are pamphlets.

Alexander, Edward Porter. *Military Memoirs of a Confederate: A Critical Narrative.* New York: Charles Scribner's Sons, 1907.

Battle-fields of the South: From Bull Run to Fredericksburgh, with Sketches of Confederate Commanders, and Gossip of the Camps. New York: John Bradburn, 1864.

Brent, Joseph L. *Memoirs of the War Between the States.* New Orleans: Fontana Printing Co., 1940.

Brown, Philip F. "Reminiscences of the War of 1861-1865." Blue Ridge Springs, Va.: privately printed, 1912.

Chamberlaine, William W. *Memoirs of the Civil War Between the Northern and Southern Sections of the United States of America, 1861 to 1865.* Washington, D.C.: Press of Byron S. Adams, 1912.

Dabney, Robert L. *The Life and Campaigns of Lieut.-Gen. Thomas J. Jackson.* New York: Blelock & Co., 1866.

Davis, Jefferson. *The Rise and Fall of the Confederate Government.* 2 vols. New York: D. Appleton & Co., 1881.

Henderson, G. F. R. *Stonewall Jackson and the American Civil War.* 2 vols. New York: Longmans, Green and Co., 1898.

Huger, Mary Esther. *The Recollection of a Happy Childhood... 1826-1848.* Edited by Mary Stevenson. Pendleton, S.C.: Published by Research and Publication Committee, Foundation for Historic Restoration in Pendleton Area, 1976.

Marshall, Charles. *An Aide-De-Camp of Lee: Being the Papers of Colonel Charles Marshall, Sometime Aide-De-Camp, Military Secretary, and Assistant Adjutant General on the Staff of Robert E. Lee, 1862-1865.* Edited by Frederick Maurice. Boston: Little, Brown & Co., 1937.

Sloan, Benjamin F. "The Merrimac and the Monitor." Columbia, S.C.: Bureau of Publications, University of South Carolina, 1926.

Smith, Gustavus W. *The Battle of Seven Pines.* New York: C. G. Crawford, 1891.

Smith, Justin H. *The War with Mexico.* 2 vols. New York: The Macmillan Co., 1919.

Swanberg, William A. *First Blood: The Story of Fort Sumter.* New York: Charles Scribner's Sons, 1957.

Taylor, Richard, *Destruction and Reconstruction: Personal Experiences of the Late War.* Edited by Richard B. Harwell. New York: Longmans, Green and Co., 1955.

Taylor, Walter H. *General Lee: His Campaigns in Virginia, 1861-1865, with Personal Reminiscences.* Norfolk: Nusbaum Book & News Co., 1906.

U.S. Congress. Senate. *Message from the President ... at the Commencement of the First Session of the Thirtieth Congress.* Senate Executive Document No. 1. Washington, D.C.: Printed by Wendell and Van Benthuysen, 1847.

Welles, T. Tileston. "The Hugers of South Carolina." New York: privately printed, 1931.

Acknowledgments

In paying this tribute to the general's memory, I owe special thanks to five notable persons: the late Miss Lucelia H. Peyton (a daughter of Corrie Peyton; see p. 120), who, through relating to me her mother's recollections of Ben Huger, kindled an interest in his life; the late Mrs. Aurelia Rutherfoord, the late Mr. John Frost, and the late Mrs. Julia Monniche for furnishing their collections of Huger's papers for my use (see bibliographical note); and Mrs. Harriot Hopkins, a daughter of Mrs. Rutherfoord, for organizing her mother's collection and for transcribing many poorly handwritten letters.

I also desire to express my sincere appreciation for the assistance rendered by Mrs. Mary B. Prior, Director of the South Carolina Historical Society; Miss Elise Pinckney, editor of the *South Carolina Historical and Geneological Magazine*; Mrs. Mary Stevenson, Director of the Research and Publication Committee of the Foundation for Historic Restoration in Pendleton Area (South Carolina); Mr. Elmer O. Parker, Mr. Karl L. Trever, and Mrs. Sarah D. Jackson of the Old Military Records Section of the National Archives; Mr. J. Harmon Smith of the Georgia Department of Archives and History; Mrs. Rosanna Hulse of Owings, Maryland, owner of the Rosanna A. Blake Library of Confederate History; Mr. William R. Hollomon, formerly Superintendent of the Richmond National Battlefield Park, and his assistants,

particularly Mr. William Kay; Mr. William E. Meuse, Jr., of
the National Park Service; Mr. Joseph M. O'Donnell, Chief of
the Archives and History Section of the West Point Library;
Mr. Michael J. McAfee, Curator of Uniforms and History of
the West Point Museum; Mrs. Dortha H. Skelton, Assistant
Reference Librarian of the College of William and Mary; Mrs.
Hazel B. Smith, former librarian of the Rego Park Branch of
the Queens Borough Public Library, New York; the late Mr.
Daniel Huger of Charleston, South Carolina; Miss Marnie
Huger of Richmond, Virginia; Mr. Nathan Magruder of Baton
Rouge, Louisiana; Miss Clermont Huger Lee of Savannah,
Georgia; Mrs. Barbara Huger of Asheville, North Carolina;
Mrs. Laura G. Frost of Charleston, South Carolina; Mr. Henri
Gerard Noordberg of Huntsville, Texas; Mr. Pete Cawthon,
Jr., of Hunt, Texas; and Mr. John L. Howells of Houston, to
whom I am especially indebted for his many years of valuable
assistance.

Index

[Rank cited in this index is the highest held by the individual prior to or during the Peninsula Campaign.]

151

Beaver Dam Creek, 68. *See also* Mechanicsville

Becham, First Lieut. Robert F., C.S.A., 56, 57

Benjamin, Judah P., 34-35, 37

Blackwater River, 31

Blakey's Mill, 47

Blanchard, Brig. Gen. Albert G., C.S.A.: at Appomattox, 46; at Seven Pines, 51, 52, 53, 59; mentioned, 81

Bledsoe, Albert T., 107

Boatswain Swamp, 68

Bottom's Bridge, 46, 83

Brackett's field, 87, 88

Brackett's Ford, 94

Bragg, Gen. Braxton, C.S.A., 25

Brent, Maj. Joseph L., C.S.A., 82, 91, 92, 102-4, 141 n. 11

Brevet: defined, 134

Brightwell's farm, 85

Buchanan, Capt. Franklin, C.S.N., 39, 40

Buchanan, James: urged by Scott to strengthen the garrisons of forts in the South, 9; his opposition, 9; urged by Scott to reinforce Anderson, 14; his reply, 14; his pledge to South Carolina, 18-19; determined to reinforce Anderson, 19; urged by Holt to reinforce Anderson, 20; sent reinforcements and provisions to Anderson, 23; and Hayne, 23-24

Bull Run. *See* Manassas

Burnside, Brig. Gen. Ambrose E., U.S.A.: held a training command in Washington, 32; assigned to organize an amphibious division, 32-33; his expedition, 34, 41; at Roanoke Island, 35, 36; spread his operations, 35-36; reinforced, 41; mentioned, 37, 44

Calhoun, John C., 134

Carter's farm, 97, 102

Castle Pinckney, S.C.: as Federal prop-

erty, 9; occupation of, 10; occupation of, advised by Anderson, 13; 15; defense of, 16; taken by state forces, 19

Cerro Gordo, Mexico, 5

Chapultepec, Mexico, 6-7, 95

Charles City Crossroads, 89, 90, 98, 106

Charles City Road, 48, 49, 50, 51, 52, 53, 54, 58, 62, 63, 66, 81, 82, 83, 85, 86, 87, 97, 103

Charleston Arsenal: commanded by Humphreys, 10; Huger sent in charge of, 11, Foster called at, for arms, 12; problem at, 15-16; occupied by state forces, 19

Charleston Daily Courier, 135 n. 19

Charleston harbor, S.C., 9, 12, 65; forts in, 9, 10, 13, 14, 16, 18, 19, 22; situation in, 10; Anderson in charge of the defenses of, 10; Huger's advice to Floyd concerning the forts in, 14; *Star of the West* repelled from, 23. *See also* Fort Johnson; Fort Moultrie; Fort Sumter; Castle Pinckney

Charleston Mercury, 19

Charleston, S.C.: birthplace of Huger, 1; 10; atmosphere in, before the Civil War, 11-12; 13, 15; secession convention convened in, 16; 17; the administration failed to understand the situation in, 18; swept with panic, 19; reaction in, when Huger declined the command of the South Carolina army, 19-20; 21; great ill-feeling in, toward Huger, 23; 24, 25, 26, 27, 65, 66, 113, 117; Huger died in, 120

Chase, Salmon P., 42, 43, 44

Chesapeake Bay, 32

Chickahominy. *See* Gaines' Mill

Chickahominy River, 46, 53, 54, 58, 66, 67, 68, 69, 80, 81, 82, 84, 109, 110

Chilton, Lieut. Col. R.H., C.S.A., 91-92, 99, 104

Chowan River, 31, 41

Churubusco, Mexico, 6

Cobb, Brig. Gen. Howell, C.S.A., 98, 105

Colston, Brig. Gen. Raleigh E., C.S.A., 41, 56, 60

Columbia, S.C., 16, 113, 120

Commissioners: South Carolina, 16, 17, 19, 20, 21, 23, 24, 25; Confederate, 26

Congress, Confederate, 37, 111, 112

Congress, warship, 39

Contreras, Mexico, 5

Court-martial: defined, 142

Court of inquiry: defined, 142

Craney Island, Va., 31, 38, 40, 44

Crew's farm. *See* Malvern Hill

Croatan Sound, N.C., 34, 35

Cumberland, warship, 39

Currituck Sound, 35

Cutts, Lieut. Col. A.S., C.S.A., 88

Darbytown Road, 81, 85, 91

Davis, Jefferson: as a cadet at West Point with Huger, 2; Pickens applied to, for an army commander, 26; Lee assigned to, as military advisor, 31, 108; Huger communicated directly with, 31–32; on the Battle of Roanoke Island, 36; his readiness to sustain Huger at Norfolk, 38–39; at Seven Pines, 58, 59, 124, 125; discussed the possibility of service in Charleston with Huger, 66; gave special instructions to Huger and Magruder, 80; at White Oak Swamp, 90, 124, 125; desired Huger's services in the West, 111, 114; requested by Huger to grant him a court-martial or a court of inquiry, 111; authorized a court of inquiry, 113, 114; requested by Frank Huger to write a statement of the reasons which led to Huger's removal from the command of his division, 123; his statement to Frank Huger, 123–24; the failure of his memory, 124; requested by Preston to write a statement, 124; his state-

ment to Preston, 125; Lizzie Huger's reflection on the statements of, 125–26; Pinckney's reaction to the statements of, 126; mentioned, 59, 114, 135–36, 138 n. 18

Davis, Mrs. Jefferson, 125

Department of Norfolk, 30, 31, 33, 38, 40, 41, 46

Department of North Carolina, 33, 67, 81

Department of the Appomattox, 46

Department of the Peninsula, 32

Department of the Rappahannock, 32

Department of the West, 113

Department of Virginia, 32

Dismal Swamp Canal, 41

Doles, Col. George, C.S.A., 80

Drewry's Bluff, Va., 45–46, 81, 110, 112

Edenton, N.C., 36

Elizabeth City, N.C., 35, 41

Elizabeth River, 31, 38, 40

Ellison's Mill. *See* Mechanicsville

Evelington Heights, Va., 106–7

Ewell, Maj. Gen. Richard S., C.S.A., 81, 83, 101

Excelsior Brigade, 67

Fair Oaks. *See* Seven Pines

Fair Oaks Station, 81, 82

Fairfield Racecourse, 55

Falling Creek, 110

Fifty-third Virginia, 52, 63

Fisher's Ford, 86, 87

Fisher's house, 97

Floyd, Maj. Gen. John B., C.S.A: sent Huger and Anderson to Charleston, 10–11; his response to Foster's request for arms, 12; urged by Anderson to send reinforcements, 12–13; his reply, 13; requested Huger to confer with Anderson, 13; Huger's advice to, 14; against reinforcement of

Hagner, Maj. Peter V., U.S.A., 26

Halls of Montezuma, 7, 95

Hampton Roads, Va., 30, 34, 39, 40, 42, 44, 45

Harden's Bluff, Va., 38

Harmony, tugboat, 112

Harpers Ferry Armory, Va. (later W. Va.), 7, 29

Harpers Ferry Arsenal, Va. (later W. Va.), 29

Harpers Ferry, Va., (later W. Va.), 29, 30

Harriet Lane, revenue cutter, 19, 23, 24

Harrison's farmhouse, 50, 57, 137

Harrison's Landing, Va., 67, 96

Hatteras Inlet, N.C., 33

Hayne, Isaac W., 23-24, 25

Heintzelman, Brig. Gen. Samuel P., U.S.A., 53, 54, 58, 67, 80, 85

Hill, Maj. Gen. A. P., C.S.A.: at Mechanicsville, 68; at Gaines' Mill, 69; at White Oak Swamp, 89-90; in the pursuit of McClellan's army, 81, 96

Hill, Maj. Gen. D. H., C.S.A.: at Seven Pines, 48,49, 50, 53, 54, 55, 56, 57, 58, 59, 60, 62, 63: at Mechanicsville, 68; at Gaines' Mill, 69; in the pursuit of McClellan's army, 81, 87, 97, 99, 106; at Malvern Hill, 101, 102; mentioned, 57, 67, 137 n. 4, 138 n. 18

Hobson's house, 86

Holmes, Maj. Gen. Theophilus H., C.S.A: in Lee's strategy, 81; at White Oak Swamp, 90-91, 92, 118; criticized for not having committed his division at White Oak Swamp and Malvern Hill, 109; sent to the Trans-Mississippi Department, 109; mentioned, 91, 95, 97

Holt, Joseph, 20

Huger, A. Eustis (son), 117

Huger, Alfred (cousin): as a volunteer assistant to Pickens,

17; Huger's letters to, 17, 24; his letter to Huger, 17-18, 19, 20, 21; his telegram to Huger, 19; informed Huger when the South Carolina representatives were to arrive in Washington, 24; saw Huger's name stigmatized in an encyclopedia, 118

Huger, Maj. Benjamin (grandfather), 1

Huger, Maj. Gen. Benjamin, C.S.A.: his aristocratic background, 1-2; as a cadet at West Point, 2-3; graduated near the top of his class while . a teenager, 3; his friendship and association with Lafayette, 2, 3, 8-9, 21; detailed on topographical duty, 3; his first European tour, 3; placed on recruiting service and then in the garrison of Ft. Trumbull, 4; his courtship and marriage, 4; promoted from second lieutenant of artillery to captain of ordnance, 4; placed in command of the Ft. Monroe Arsenal, 4; became a member of the ordnance board of the War Department, 4-5; his second European tour, 5; served as the chief of ordnance and artillery to Scott and commanded a siege train, 5; at Vera Cruz, 5; at Molino del Rey, 6; at Chapultepec, 6-7; in Scott's report, 7; given Santa Anna's spurs by Scott, 7; honored by the army and his native state, 7; resumed command of the Ft. Monroe Arsenal and again served on the ordnance board, 7; served as the superintendent of the Harpers Ferry Armory, 7; assumed the dual role of commander of the Pikesville Arsenal and inspector of U.S. foundries, 7; promoted to major, 7; on secession, 8, 17, 20, 22; Lafayette's letter to, 8-9; selected as ambassador in charge of the Charleston Arsenal, 11; assumed command of the arsenal, 11; his long friendship with Anderson, 11, 22, 24; offered the position of commander in chief of the South Carolina army, 11,

20; at Malvern Hill, 98, 102–5, 106, 141 n. 11; the observation of his chief of artillery, 101; criticized by the troops and press throughout the campaign for his "slowness," 109; relieved of command and given an empty title, 109; Lee's betrayal of, 110, 120, 126; his withdrawal from Malvern Hill and encampment, 110; turned the command of his division over to R. H. Anderson, 110; his once brilliant reputation ruined, 110; stories multiplied from his alleged failures, 110–11; accused by some of treason, 111; viciously attacked in Congress, 111; offered to resign from the army, 111, 120; urged by Randolph not to leave the service, 111, 120; his services desired by Davis in the West, 111, 114; directed his efforts to vindicating himself to the public, 111; applied for copies of Johnston's and Longstreet's Seven Pines reports, 111; requested Davis to grant him a court-martial, 111; his investigation of Seven Pines discouraged by Johnston, 111, 113; received a letter from Tattnall, 113; his reply, 112–13; his faith in the power of truth, xi, 112, 116, 126; his answer from Davis to his request for a court-martial, 113; his renewals of his request, 113, 114; ordered on a tour of ordnance establishments, 113; asked that the court be assembled before Johnston was assigned to any distant command, 113; answered that the state of the service would not permit the granting of his request, 113; began an inspection of artillery and ordnance stores, 113; received orders to make a similar tour through the Trans-Mississippi Department, 113; his letter from Frank Huger, 113–14; his reply, 114; in the Trans-Mississippi region, 114–15; prevented from renewing his application for court, 115; wanted no part in postwar controversies,

116, 122, 126; would not return to South Carolina while its government was in alien hands, 116; settled in Baltimore and entered business, 116; the deaths of his wife and eldest son, 116–17; moved to Virginia and lived in obscurity, 117; stayed with Lizzie Huger in Charleston, 117; his conversation with Hunt about Porter, 118, 120; his name stigmatized in *The American Cyclopaedia* and the efforts to correct it, 118–19, 122–23; his illness and relapse, 119; Lizzie Huger's memoir of her interview with, 119–20, 123; his death, 120; the reactions to his death, 120–21; his funeral 122; the proposed biographical vindication of, 123–26; Davis's statements on, 123–26

Huger, Mrs. Benjamin (Celly): her courtship and marriage, 4; called "beautiful little madam" by Lee, 110; rumored to be sister of Mrs. Wool, 110; her illness and death, 116–17; buried in Baltimore, 117; mentioned, 113, 115, 116, 122

Huger, Capt. Benjamin, Jr., C.S.A. (son), 115, 116–17, 122

Huger, Celestine Pinckney (Celly) (daughter): lived with Huger at Gordonsdale, 117; her marriage, 117; informed of Huger's death and her reaction 120; Peyton's letter to, 120; Meta Huger's letter to, 120–21; on public controversy, 122; mentioned, 124, 125

Huger, Cleland Kinloch (brother): Huger stayed with, in Charleston, 11; and Gist's telegram, 13–14; his telegrams to Huger, 17, 20; warned by Huger to expect attacks against the latter, 110; mentioned, 118, 140

Huger, Daniel (great-great-grandfather), 1

Huger, Elizabeth Pinckney (Lizzie) (sister): Huger stayed with, in Charleston, 117; became aware of the extent to which Huger had been maligned, 117–18; struck by Huger's conversation with Hunt about Porter, 118; on the encyclopedic entry stigmatizing Huger's name, 118, 119; her memoir after interviewing Huger, 119-20, 123; suggested that a biographical vindication of Huger be written, 123; wrote the general biographical portion, 123; encouraged the vindication to be written, 126; on Lee's betrayal of Huger, 110, 120, 126; her reply to Frank Huger concerning the impossibility of vindicating Huger, 126; mentioned, 134 n. 2, 140 n. 20

Huger, Francis Kinloch (father): background of, 1; attempted to rescue Lafayette, 1; on tour with Lafayette, 2; his friendship with Calhoun despite their differing political views, 134; mentioned, 3, 8, 9

Huger, Capt. Frank, C.S.A. (son): his letter to Huger, 113–14; Huger's reply to, 114; his efforts to vindicate Huger, 118, 123, 126; wired the news of Huger's death to his sister, 120; requested Davis to write a statement of the reasons which led to Huger's removal from the command of his division, 123; Davis's statement to, 123–24; mentioned, 122, 125, 146

Huger, Harriott Lucas (mother), 1

Huger, Meta D. (niece), 120

Huger, Thomas Pinckney (son). See Pinckney, First Lieut. Thomas

Humphreys, Francis C.: in command of the Charleston arsenal, 10; in arms issue with Foster, 15–16; surrendered, 19; in Huger's counsel, 22

Hunt, Col. Henry J., U.S.A.: Huger's conversation with, about Porter, 118; in Lizzie Huger's memoir, 120

Jackson, Maj. Gen. Thomas J. (Stonewall), C.S.A.: at Harpers Ferry, 29; in the Shenandoah Valley, 53; in Lee's strategies,

67–68, 68–69, 81; at Mechanicsville, 68; at Gaines' Mill, 69; in the pursuit of McClellan's army, 81, 82, 83–84, 96, 98, 106, 139 n. 6; at White Oak Swamp, 89, 93–95, 110, 118, 140 n. 20; at Malvern Hill, 98, 99, 100, 101, 102, 103; denounced and his command reduced after the Seven Days' Battles, 109; mentioned, 87

James Adger, ship, 12, 13

James River, 29, 30, 38, 42, 43, 44, 45, 46, 66, 67, 81, 90, 96, 98, 110

Jenkins, Col. Micah, C.S.A., 95

Johnston, Gen. Joseph E., C.S.A.: assumed command of the forces on the peninusla to oppose McClellan, 40; decided to withdraw up the peninsula, 41; ordered Huger to abandon Norfolk, 41; ordered Huger's command to join his army, 46; at Seven Pines, 48, 49, 50, 51, 52, 53, 54–59, 61–63; his report on Seven Pines, 62–63, 64, 111, 122; discouraged Huger's investigation of Seven Pines, 111, 113; sent to the West, 109, 113; his book searched by Huger for a retraction, 119; mentioned, 45, 50, 114, 123, 126, 138 n. 15, 138 n. 18, 141 n. 1

Jordan's Ford, 85, 86

Kearny, Brig. Gen. Philip, U.S.A., 85–86

Keyes, Brig. Gen. Erasmus D., U.S.A.: at Seven Pines, 53, 54, 55, 58, 63; at King's Schoolhouse, 67

King's Schoolhouse, 67

Lafayette, Marquis de: entertained by Huger's grandfather, 1; rescued by Huger's father, 1; met by Huger at West Point during his tour of the United States; 2; visited by Huger in Paris, 3; wrote letters of introduction for Huger, 3; his views on an American civil war, 8-9, 21

Lee, Gen. Robert E., C.S.A.: named

commander in chief in Virginia, 30; his inspection of Norfolk, 30; his long friendship with Huger, 30, 66, 110; asked Huger to take command of the Department of Norfolk, 30; his orders to Huger, 30; his early Confederate positions and rank, 31; his reputation damaged by Wise, 33; succeeded Johnston at Seven Pines, 53; Huger's letter to, 60; forwarded the letter to Longstreet, 60; his friendship with Longstreet, 65, 109; his opinion of Huger before and after Seven Pines, 66, 142 n. 5; ordered the construction of earthworks, 66; his strategies, 67-69, 81, 96; his operations north of the Chickahominy River, 67-69; in the pursuit of McClellan's army, 81, 82, 83, 84, 85, 87, 90, 98, 99, 106-7; tactical errors caused by his map, 90, 98-99, 108-9; at White Oak Swamp, 91, 92, 124, 125; at Malvern Hill, 98, 99-100, 101-2, 103, 104, 105-6; responsible for the failure of every major battle of the Seven Days, 108-9; never bore the repercussions for his blunders, 109; failed in his attempts to destroy McClellan's army, 109; made Longstreet his second in command, 109; his betrayal of Huger, 110, 120, 126; did not verbally censure Huger, 111, 120; his report of the Seven Days' Battles cited, 110, 122; mentioned, 41, 45, 59, 65, 91, 97, 98, 99, 138 n. 15, 141 n. 11

Lee, Capt. Sidney Smith, C.S.N.: given instructions from Mallory to delay the naval evacuation of Norfolk, 41; Huger's message to , 43, 112; Tattnall's flag lieutenant sent to confer with Huger and, 44; in Huger's letter to Tattnall, 112

Letcher, Gov. John, 30

Lincoln, Abraham: as a presidential candidate, 9; his election incited South Carolina to secede, 9; his Inaugural Address, 26; his message to Pickens, 26; in

Huger's resignation, 27; in Huger's letter to Scott, 27; his unwillingness to leave Washington exposed by McDowell's removal, 40; at Fort Monroe, 42; ordered war vessels to harrass Confederate ships on James River, 42; directed Wool to capture Norfolk, 42; ordered a reconnaissance of Huger's batteries at Sewell's Point, 42; ordered a landing at Willoughby's Point, 43; toured Norfolk, 44

Long Bridge Road, 81, 89, 90, 91, 96, 97, 98

Longstreet, Maj. Gen. James, C.S.A.: at Seven Pines, 50-51, 52-53, 54-64, 114, 138 n. 18, 142 n. 15; his claim of seniority over Huger, 50-51, 55, 57, 59, 107, 114, 138 n. 15; his report on Seven Pines, 62, 63, 64, 111, 113, 119, 122; his general orders, 63-64; his retraction, 64, 119; pretended to be second in command of the army, 65, 91, 96; his second attempt to rid the army of Huger, 66; in Lee's strategies, 68, 69, 81, 110; at Mechanicsville, 68; at Gaines' Mill, 69; in the pursuit of McClellan's army, 96, 97, 106; at White Oak Swamp, 88, 89-90, 91, 92, 95; at Malvern Hill, 98, 99-100, 102; his friendship with Lee, 65, 109; became second in command in Virginia, 109; became the senior lieutenant general in the Confederate States, 109-10; mentioned, 110, 114, 117, 126, 140 n. 21

Lorring, Maj. Gen. W. W., C.S.A., 46

McCall, Brig. Gen. George A., U.S.A., 68, 89

McClellan, Maj. Gen. George B., U.S.A.: appointed to command the Army of the Potomac, 32; temporarily succeeded Scott, 32; his plan to capture Richmond, 32; assigned Burnside to organize an amphibious division, 32; his troops landed at Ft. Monroe and